By Reason of Insanity

By Reason

The David Michael Krueger Story

of Insanity

MARK BOURRIE

HOUNSLOW PRESS
A MEMBER OF THE DUNDURN GROUP
TORONTO & OXFORD

Hounslow Press
A member of the Dundurn Group

Canadian Cataloguing in Publication Data

Bourrie, Mark, 1957–
    By reason of insanity

ISBN 0-88882-196-4

1. Krueger, David Michael. 2. Murderers – Ontario – Biography.
3. Brockville Psychiatric Hospital – Case studies. I. Title.

HV6248.K78E68 1997   364.15 ' 23 ' 092   C97-931825-4

1 2 3 4 5 TH 01 00 99 98 97

We acknowledge the support of the **Canada Council for the Arts** for our publishing program. We also acknowledge the support of the **Ontario Arts Council** and the **Book Publishing Industry Development Program** of the **Department of Canadian Heritage**.

THE CANADA COUNCIL | LE CONSEIL DES ARTS
FOR THE ARTS | DU CANADA
SINCE 1957 | DEPUIS 1957

Care has been taken to trace the ownership of copyright material used in this book. The author and the publisher welcome any information enabling them to rectify any references or credit in subsequent editions.

Front cover photograph: Lynn Ball, *The Ottawa Citizen*

Hounslow Press
8 Market Street
Suite 200
Toronto, Ontario, Canada
M5E 1M6

Hounslow Press
73 Lime Walk
Headington, Oxford
England
OX3 7AD

Hounslow Press
250 Sonwil Drive
Buffalo, NY
U.S.A. 14225

ACKNOWLEDGEMENTS

This book couldn't have been written without the help of David Michael Krueger, who generously provided me access to his voluminous clinical file and sat for hundreds of hours of interviews. Thanks, too, to Dr. Elliot Barker; Dr. Russell Fleming, George Kytayko, Dan Parle, and numerous other staff at Oak Ridge and the Mental Health Centre Penetanguishene; Justice Douglas Carruthers of the Ontario Review Board; Judge Robert Main, Ontario Court; Crown Attorney Andrejs Berzins (Ottawa Region); lawyer Dan Brodsky; the staff of the Penetanguishene Mental Health Centre reference library; David Rabinovitch, Christian Magee and Victor Hoffman; journalists Carey Moran, Paul Welch and Debi Levy of the *Midland Free Press*; David Dauphinee of the *London Free Press*; Kate Harries, Dave Annis, John Ferri, Dave Ellis, Steve Tustin, Fred Kuntz, Kelly Hudson, Mark Harrison and Susan Pigg of the *Toronto Star*; Michael Fitz-James of *Canadian Lawyer*; Beth Marlin of *Law Times*; William Walker, Chris Cobb and Scott Anderson of the *Ottawa Citizen*; Mike Therrien of the *Ottawa Sun*; staff at the Library of Parliament; Kady O'Malley, Kathleen O'Hara, John Cruppi, Mike Scandiffio and the rest of my colleagues at the Parliamentary Press Gallery; and Tony Hawke and Kirk Howard of Dundurn-Hounslow.

A special thanks to my family, especially my wife, Marion, and Dawn and Ralph Varney, for their support.

For
Gary Morris,
Wayne Mallette,
Carole Voyce,
Dennis Kerr
and their families.

CONTENTS

A Note About Names

The subject of this book has lived with a number of names. I have chosen to call him Peter Woodcock, his birth name, in the early years of his life. He's called David Michael Krueger from the time that he legally changes his name. David Michael Krueger and Peter Woodcock are very much the same person.

A few names have been changed. A youth whose wrongful conviction is recounted has his privacy protected. So, too, do several Oak Ridge inmates who are mentioned in passing and have now been released.

INTRODUCTION

Every day or two, the phone rings in my home. The little Call Display window on the phone shows the words "Long Distance". When I pick it up, a computer voice begins the collect call chant. "You have a collect call from," it says, pausing for the voice of the caller. Then there's the polite little message, "is this a good time to call?" or there's a bit of quick gossip from Oak Ridge, or there's simply the word "Mike". If it's "Mike", I usually accept the call. My wife never does. When David Michael Krueger calls, she puts the phone down. She wants to stay out of the world of the Oak Ridge hospital for the "criminally insane" in Penetanguishene, and its resident murderers. Lately, we've installed a phone with a special ring, a compromise in the ongoing dispute about whether the Kruegers of the world should have any presence in our home.

The calls come from an old pay phone at the end of Krueger's ward. Down the hall is his cell. It's about the size of a small kitchen or a large washroom, institutional grey, with a high ceiling and a small window facing an exercise yard. There's a little bed, a table with a short wave radio, a television that my mother bought at a Sears when I was a teenager, and that I passed on to Krueger two decades later. There's also a boom box with a CD player, some books about trains, and a collection of photos of old Toronto streetcars.

There are no reminders of his crimes: the murder of those three children in Toronto in 1956-1957, the often vicious sexual assaults of dozens more during the same period of time, and the brutal slaughter of Dennis Kerr. Three murders qualifies a person for that now-fashionable title of serial killer. That dubious achievement is something that Krueger has recently started to wallow in. He even talks of becoming the world's first serial killer science fiction writer. He thinks he would make a fortune, and he may be right.

Every day is dull in Oak Ridge, even when the place is enveloped in some new scandal or controversy involving patients' rights or the bizarre actions of inmates and some of its staff. A visit from anyone is a treasure for inmates of the Penetanguishene institution. When I leave, Krueger always asks when I am going to come back. When I come back, he wants to know if I'll return soon. In the first year I knew him, I lived almost within sight of Oak Ridge. I could look out the windows of my home and see Georgian Bay's winter squalls roll over the peninsula where Krueger lives, hiding the place in a cloud of snow.

The first time I talked with Krueger was in July, 1993. I had wanted to interview him, along with any other patients who were willing to be part of a book on the sixty-year-old Oak Ridge institution. I didn't think he would talk to anyone after the nasty press he got for the Brockville murder. I called Oak Ridge and left a message for him. The attendant said he would "pass it on to him if he's here", as a paean to the concept of patient confidentiality. About five minutes later, my phone rang and Krueger's mellow monotone voice came on. I told him I was writing a book about the history of his psychiatric prison and wanted to talk to him since he had been there longer than anyone, including most staff. I also let him know that I would ask about his own life and his murders.

"That's fine, I would love to be interviewed," he cooed, "but there are things about me that may terrify you and I don't know if you'll be able to handle them."

I said I had some background on his life, and, though it might be hard, I could probably take what ever he told me without throwing up or strangling him.

"Good," he said. "When are you coming over?"

I said the next day, 10 a.m.

"There are people in here who want me dead. I can't leave my ward. You'll have to come in and sit with me in the sun room. It will be good because you can see how I live."

That was fine.

"'Til tomorrow, au revoir," he said.

Staff nixed the idea of us meeting on his ward, so we talked in the Oak Ridge visitor's centre, a large, cafeteria-style room that's open to all of the patients. One of the nurse-guards brought him to the door of the centre and just left him with me. There we were: him looking like a little half-blind Don Rickles or Art Buchwald in a checked shirt and shorts, me watching quite carefully for the people who wanted him dead. I turned on a miniature tape recorder and stuck the wrong end under his nose.

I had expected to see him only once, for a few hours.

Instead, I kept coming back, and the phone calls began. Once, he pretended to be the computerized recorded message from the telephone company, asking if I would accept a collect call. Another time, he told me he had just watched a Bugs Bunny cartoon about Hansel and Gretl. The evil witch was about to cook the fat little Teutonic kids up and she had a stack of cook books to help her do it right.

"Only someone like me could appreciate the humour in that cartoon," he said.

Most of the time, he seems like a normal, if slightly pompous, middle-aged man. He suffers from problems with his teeth and he squints when he looks at things that are more than a few metres away, but otherwise, he appears to be fairly normal. Only when the conversation turns to murder, the "tragedies", does he seem strange. The weirdness lies in the fact that he's so calm, so distant from his own vile crimes. He talks about the murders as though he's discussing last night's TV programs. Sometimes he whispers, as though there's something about the murders that hasn't been written down in his huge psychiatric file or wasn't entered in the court record. Other times, he pretends to show insight about his crimes.

The logic was sometimes as skewed as "why did they go after that Son of Sam guy in New York? After all, it was the dog that was crazy." After a while, he lets it show that the crimes, at worst, have been an inconvenience for him. At best, they have been a ticket to a life of nurture at the bosom of the state, without major cares; a steady dose of excitement that shatters the institutional calm; protection from an outside world that has become more alien and frightening with each passing day; and lots of male company to manipulate and seduce.

There are bizarre moments during our visit, like the time that I carried a greasy "Texas breakfast" from his favorite restaurant into the visitors' centre and had to listen to Krueger carve away at a tough steak on a styrofoam tray. While he hacked at the chunk of meat, the child-killer peered at a toddler playing just a few feet away.

Krueger is a lonely man. Sometimes newspaper work prevented me from showing up and there was no way to call him. He would wait for the guards to take him down, but eventually he would realize he had been stood up. Those were bad days for both of us, and I would apologize profusely. Institutional life is very lonely.

"It's alright," he would say with a giggle, during our next visit. "I'm not going to kill you."

Then he would tell me the gossip in Oak Ridge, the rumours about other patients and the staff. He would make up stories that the Oak Ridge inmates had applied to the Canadian Society for the Prevention of Cruelty to Animals to close the place down or at least improve the quality of the food.

Often he's broke. His $112 a month comfort allowance doesn't go far. He doesn't smoke anymore and couldn't afford cigarettes if he wanted to start again. Most of his money goes for coffee, music tapes, a very few clothes, a rare compact disc or a book. I lent him $10 to get him through the last week of November, 1993. He was gleeful and promised to return the money. It bought more for him than it would have for me, so I let him keep it. I also bought him lunch once in a while. That started a slight dependence. Every few months, he needed $5, or at least asked me to pay for his coffee during our visits. That, despite rumours in Oak Ridge, has been the extent of our financial dealings.

In 1995, when he suddenly came into a bit of money, he could finally be generous. He wanted to give me an antique radio for a wedding present. He spent $600 in one week on food for the people on his ward. The generosity was quite real: it buys him attention, and he gives until it hurts. The cash, $2,250, was going fast. I told him to hang onto his money, that it would be irreplaceable when it was gone, but within a few months, there was nothing left.

One day, I brought my dog with me. Animals aren't allowed in Oak Ridge, so I parked about three metres from a visitor centre window. Krueger could see the dog through the thick glass and got a better look at him when guards made me move the car. I let the dog out to run around, then looked over to see Krueger and a janitor watching through a barred window. When I went back inside, he was bouncing and chatty. My dog was surely the most beautiful creature he had ever seen, he said.

One winter afternoon, two Metro Toronto plainclothes cops were dragging a chained and shackled black man up the front steps of Oak Ridge. Krueger squinted through the glass and muttered: "They're bringing more niggers and pakis to this place all the time. It's really going downhill."

His racism doesn't extend to native people. Oak Ridge is home to several middle-aged men from Indian reserves who have fried their brains with booze, drugs and solvents and have ended up killing people. Krueger seems to be friends with most of them. Among the people he really warmed to recently was an Inuit man who was shipped to Oak Ridge for tests after he was charged with killing two men who had raped his sister. For months, Krueger watched over and worried about this young man, who barely spoke English. In the end, the man was acquitted of all charges and set free. He was one of the few people who pass through Oak Ridge who are genuinely innocent of the crime they are charged with.

Krueger has many semi-secret obsessions: young men, children, maybe young women, though perhaps that's just fake macho talk. Those obsessions, he's learned, are best kept to himself unless he's sure the person he shares them with will not use them against him. He has two quite public obsessions, the

Toronto Transit Commission's streetcars, and the now-defunct Russian imperial family.

The Romanovs fit into Krueger's power fantasy system. Eventually, because of that fantasy, I was able to get an idea of how his mind works. The thought of the absolute power of the last Tsar thrills a man who is powerless. The might and majesty of this weakling king, who was able to kill without sanction, is an inspiration to any killer geek. Krueger has kept up on the research that has been done at the Romanov remains found in 1990 at Ekaterinburg. He knows how old the two youngest Romanov children would be if they had survived, and about the various pretenders. I suspect, in his fantasy life, he is one of those Romanovs.

The fantasy surrounding the Toronto Transit Commission goes back farther, and is harder to fathom. The idea of a scrawny, pimply adolescent timing busses and streetcars suggests, I suppose, that he was trying to create or pretend to oversee some sort of order in the chaos in his life. The streetcars and the busses were the most impressive vehicles around in those pre-Boeing 747 days. They would impress any boy. The fantasy lasted through his years at the school for troubled kids in Kingston, and Krueger brought his collection of Toronto Transit Commission timetables to Oak Ridge, where he sat in his cell during the 1960s with a watch and Perly street guides, keeping track of the movements of the old Witte streetcars.

If he hadn't been a killer, Krueger might have been happy as a rail traffic controller. He was scandalized that my sister had worked as a train dispatcher, essentially getting paid to do what Krueger was is so willing to do for free, and was troubled by the fact that she had given up the job rather than move from northern Ontario to Toronto. The idea of a woman with power over trains was, to him, quite incredible, and I don't think he believed me when I told him that the railway had, indeed, stopped discriminating against the people he called "the weaker sex".

"Though, of course," he added, "girls are stronger than boys, and much more difficult to subdue."

So, if David Michael Krueger, who readily admits he has "presided over four deaths" is happy enough tucked away in a $400-a-day Ontario government cocoon on the shores of Georgian Bay, would he want to let an outsider, a writer, no less, into his life? After all, no one could write about his life without describing the "tragedies", and he loathes the embarrassment they cause. Other writers had come to see him, people like Judy Steed from the *Globe and Mail*, and Dini Petti, the talk show host, but he had always required them to sign a form saying they wouldn't divulge his crimes. With me, it was all on the record, and within half an hour of meeting him, my hands were clammy and my chair seemed electrified. I had to get up and walk around, look out the window, sort through the cards in my wallet. He was not an easy man to listen to.

There were a few superficial reasons for Krueger's decision to let me interview him off and on, for more than four years. A big icebreaker was the fact that, as a student, I had worked for a railway and shared his love of trains. We had mutual dislike of some of the Oak Ridge staff and the psychopathic patients who have the real power there. In the newspapers, Krueger was getting all of the blame for the Brockville murder. An inquest into Kerr's death was coming up and he wanted to tell his side. Amazingly, he wasn't being called as a witness. Probably the main reason, however, was the fact that he is lonely, like any other shut-in. My visit was the first one he had in about a year, since the lawyers in the Brockville murder had finished their work.

Something else that bothered him was the media speculation about his new name. Reporters naturally believed the change from Woodcock to Krueger was made to honour Freddie Krueger, the anti-hero of the Nightmare on Elm Street movies. In fact, he had made the name change in 1982, two years before the first of the Elm Street movies came out. Krueger told me this on our first meeting. He badly wanted me to believe it, so I checked with the lawyer who did the paperwork. Robert Main is a provincial court judge now. He remembers making the application in 1982, shortly before he was appointed to the bench. As well, the paperwork in

Krueger's file backs both of them up. The name change is legal and binding, paid for by Ontario's legal aid program. I suspect the writers of the movie and the killer picked the name because of its nasty, guttural qualities. Still, it's a hell of a coincidence.

Despite his anger at the idea that he'd plagiarized his name, Krueger still wallows in its notoriety.

"Some people ask me if I'm related to Freddie Krueger. I say He's my cousin. He's not really the black sheep of the family. His three sons, Mean, Vicious and Cruel, are."

Inside Oak Ridge, the Krueger name draws little attention. After all, most of the one hundred and twenty inmates of the institution are murderers. Power inside Oak Ridge comes from personal charisma and physical strength. Those inmates who want to rule spend their time working out in the institution's gym or on their own exercise equipment. Those who want protection and friendship from the elite provide services to them. One man, a serial killer from southwestern Ontario, runs a cut-rate bootleg movie video rental business, with more than two thousand titles in stock. The movies range from X-rated porn and slaughter movies to kids' films. Another inmate, a serial arsonist, did Freedom of Information searches and acted as a jailhouse lawyer until he was transferred. The less imaginative have only their bodies or their cigarettes as currency. An inmate will gain a few points for standing lookout while two patients have sex. Others, like Krueger, try to win influence with their generosity. He's got a long way to go to get back into the elite social circle, since his last murder slowed transfers from Oak Ridge for several years and brought the kind of publicity that helps keep psychopaths locked up, no matter how well behaved they are.

Living in peace with other inmates goes a long way toward making a stay at Oak Ridge tolerable. The institution is far less dangerous than a federal prison, where most of Oak Ridge's inmates, including its elite, would be at the bottom of the pecking order. No Oak Ridge inmate has ever killed or maimed a fellow patient (though Krueger came close to committing a murder, once, and has been attacked a couple of times). There are a few punch-outs between inmates, but they're quickly broken up by guards. Sometimes, inmates assault the staff. Years ago, that would have brought vicious beating down on the miscreant inmate. Now, the guards are much more likely to lay an assault charge and file for Workers' Compensation. There have been allegations of guards needlessly brutalizing the inmates. Several police investigations have been conducted, but nothing has been proven.

It's not an air of menace that hangs over Oak Ridge, it's more an atmosphere of boredom. No one is compelled to work or take part in programs, so people who are seriously disturbed, depressed, lazy or living in a cloud of hopelessness tend to sit in lounges watching TV or stand, chain smoking, in the halls in front of their cells. The swimming pool built a few years ago is empty most of the time. It gets the most use on Sundays, when people from the town of Penetanguishene, which has no recreational facilities to speak of, are allowed in through a side door and the hallway to the rest of the institution is sealed off.

Krueger gives mixed reviews to the food in Oak Ridge. He describes the Swedish meatballs as "greasy technicolour nightmares". As for the chicken cutlets, "these things have to be seen to be believed". The liver and onions are good, he says. It's one of their better meals. The baked herbal chicken "would put Colonel Sanders to shame". Of course, Krueger's fine dining expertise is limited, since he hasn't eaten an unsupervised meal outside of a psychiatric institution in nearly forty years and the most money he's ever made is about $150 a month.

He says however, "I've eaten in restaurants up and down Highway 401, from St. Thomas to Montreal (usually on trips to court or to other institutions). I've tried to find this kind of recipe, and the restaurants along the highway just can't duplicate it. Nothing else they make comes close." He knows what he'll be eating on any given day, months in advance, since Oak Ridge's menu plan is on a four-week rotation that almost never changes. This is probably comforting to a man whose idea of fun is to keep track of busses and streetcars.

"They have a relatively good menu for three weeks of the cycle," he said during a 1994 visit. "This week we get roast beef

Sunday, baked herbal chicken on Monday. Then the next two days it's guts, it's swill, it's garbage. Next Thursday, it will be cold turkey. Then Friday, it will be steak night, which is good. Sirloin, likely. They used to be rib-eye. There's no T-bones because the bones might be used to make slingshots (actually, the bones are easily made into daggers). Once, a farmer came in and asked for the swill that was thrown out from the kitchen. He wanted to feed it to his pigs. But I think we got the leftovers, and the pigs got whatever we were supposed to get. Anyway, the Society for the Prevention of Cruelty to Animals put an end to it because they said it was unhygienic to feed the stuff they serve here to animals."

In the summer of 1993, several steak nights were cancelled because of government cutbacks, causing dismay throughout the institution. After the election of Mike Harris' Tories, the cooking staff lost their jobs and food was brought in from another hospital. Krueger likes it better than the old Oak Ridge food, but the portions are smaller. Second helpings are no longer allowed, and Krueger complained through the winter of 1997 that he goes to bed hungry. When the food is really bad, Krueger and the other inmates send out for hamburgers, Chinese food and pizzas, which are delivered to Oak Ridge from Penetanguishene restaurants by nervous delivery boys or by cab drivers who are happy to get the work. Restaurant owners in Penetanguishene vie for Oak Ridge's business, since some good customers, those collecting Canada Pension Plan disability cheques, have as much as $800 a month to spend on whatever they want. Some inmates send out for all of their meals.

On many of my visits, I brought food or paid for disgusting microwaved hotdogs or hamburgers from the canteen where we always had our meetings. As often as I could, I brought hamburgers from Ken Cowan's pool hall on Penetanguishene's main street. Cowan is a friendly guy who has fed half of Penetang on credit. And the credit of the half of Penetanguishene that he has fed is rather dubious. Krueger praised Cowan's fresh, home-made hamburgers and passed the word to other Oak Ridge patients. Cowan had never gone after Oak Ridge's take-out market, but within days of the first burger shipment, he was getting phone-in orders.

One time, I got into trouble with security because I didn't tell them there was a plastic fork in the burger bag. No eating utensils, plastic or otherwise, can be brought into Oak Ridge. They are on the same list as Rolaids, cough medications, glass bottles, and the more predictable contraband such as guns, knives, explosives and street drugs. Visitors entering the institution have to pass through a set of barred steel doors, then sign in and wear a plastic visitor ID card. Anyone who isn't known to the guards can expect to be asked to go through a metal detector and will be warned about taking in contraband. New visitors are escorted down a corridor to the large, bright room where inmates entertain their guests. Eventually, regular visitors pass through the steel doors and walk the corridor on their own, through the crowd of inmates who loiter in the hallway. The guards phone the ward where the patient who is being visited lives, and he is sent down to the visitors' centre. Usually, visitors have to wait a half an hour or more before their host arrives, with nothing to do but read pamphlets from Alcoholics Anonymous or wonder why the Canadian Mental Health Association, which works so hard to dispel the mythology of mental illness, sells nuts in its three gum machines in the visitors' centre.

Since only the guards wear uniforms (dark pants and light blue shirts and a dark blue tie), visitors can quite easily tell who the inmates are. Most look like poor people you would see on any downtown street in Canada. In fact, the people who live in Oak Ridge appear, and for the most part, talk, like men who were grabbed at random from a shabby bar or a bad restaurant. It's important to remember that no one is stamped with an "M" brand for murderer or an "R" brand for rapist. The polite man at the coffee counter in the visitors' centre could be the rapist whose trial you followed in the papers a few years ago, the serial killer who terrorized some rural corner of your province or the child murderer who was the focus of a long manhunt. Once in Oak Ridge, he's part of the community, adjusting as quickly as he can to an artificial world where he can live in asylum, in the real sense of the word.

Inside that asylum, that protected place, inmates can pick and choose what they want from the outside world. Most have VCRs, and murder movies rent well from serial killer Chris Magee's bootleg stash that the hospital keeps in a basement storage room, or from local rental stores (again, brought by taxi). Each ward has two TV rooms. One is dedicated to movie channels, while the other shows sports. Books are rare, but computers are becoming common on Ward 04 and Ward 02, the two floors dedicated to long-term psychopaths, or, in the parlance of Oak Ridge, people suffering from "personality disorders". Modems and the Internet aren't available yet. There aren't enough phone lines. Soon, if the inmates get their way, they'll be online, creating a generation of something right out of Hollywood: serial killers surfing the 'Net, homicidal cyberpunks. These days, the reality is less ominous. Most of the computers are used for games or for writing.

Krueger's tastes are frozen in the 1950s, which makes sense, considering that's the time when he was yanked out of society and locked away. He listens to short wave radio, likes the Metropolitan Opera on the CBC, and tunes into radio talk shows, mostly ones hosted by right-wingers. His recorded music is mostly classical, a taste that no one else on his ward shares.

His idea of high humor is the Royal Canadian Air Farce, and he's been suffering loudly since Dave Broadfoot left the show. The recent resurfacing of Stompin' Tom Connors has brought him some delight, too. Rush Limbaugh is a welcome voice in Krueger's cell. With the incredible amount of time he has on his hands, there's opportunity to look for new heros and fresh electronic friends on the AM, FM and short wave bands. Oak Ridge keeps him locked up in idleness, fourteen waking hours a day, seven days a week, month after month, year after year.

Until 1996, Krueger didn't work in any Oak Ridge shops because he believed any money he made would be deducted from his $112-a-month provincial comfort allowance. Then, in the fall of that year, he got a part-time job in the institution to help cover the cost of our phone conversations. This was an unrequested bit of generosity that put a substantial dent in my phone bill. In return, I tried to travel from my home near Ottawa to Penetanguishene more often.

In theory, Krueger should be spending his time, the time that taxpayers pay for at such an incredible rate, in some sort of therapy so that he can either get out or move to a place that is less of a financial burden on the public. That's not going to happen. No treatment is offered to Krueger. The vogue among most psychiatrists now is that psychopaths, people with no feelings at all for others, are untreatable. Since the 1960s and 1970s, when Krueger was one of the guinea pigs used in treatment experiments at Oak Ridge, psychiatry has given up on him and his ilk. Even if someone came up with a new treatment idea, Krueger could refuse to take part. He probably would, unless it was easy.

Despite reams of reports that say Krueger only takes treatment when he thinks it will help him get out, he claims to have real curiosity about the nature of his illness. He wonders if there are multiple personalities at work inside him, ones that take over when he's stressed and lash out by killing. He hasn't suggested the idea to a psychiatrist. In fact, in the first two years after he was returned to Oak Ridge in 1992, he never saw a psychiatrist at all. He says he had a brain scan at the Royal Ottawa Hospital in 1985 that found a ridge of scar tissue in the area of the brain that deals with mathematics. He says it also explains "some of the bizarre aspects of my logic". Otherwise, except for the multiple personality theory, he has no ideas to offer about his madness, after nearly forty years in mental institutions.

So after all of these years, what have we got for the time and money spent on Krueger? A half-blind four-time killer with limited social skills, a man who can't drive a car, cook a meal or do a load of laundry. We've kept, as something of a pet of the state, a man who has never paid income tax, balanced a chequebook, filled out a job application form, or slept in a house by himself. The idea of freedom is terrifying to Krueger. Likely, his forty years behind bars is about two-thirds of his imprisonment. Barring any new diseases (and he seems to be in great health), Krueger will likely live at least another twenty years. There's almost no doubt that the time will be spent in the Oak Ridge hospital or a maximum-security ward in another institution.

So we're left paying to keep this bizarre man who offers himself as "a study specimen".

"I do have shallowness of emotional response," he says. "It's entirely situational. Whatever I am, I am a product of Oak Ridge. I grew up here. My personality reflects the influences here, and I'm accused of having no morality, which is a fair assessment, because my morality is whatever the system allows, whatever I can get away with. In a setting like this, the people to fear are the staff, not God."

INITIATION DAY

It was hot and muggy on Saturday, 13 July, 1991, when Bruce Hamill, a physically and mentally twisted young man, rode the elevator down from his eighth floor apartment in suburban Ottawa and headed for a bus stop. A few minutes later, he was on his way to the capital's modern black steel and glass railway station. As the bus carried him closer to the train terminal, he could see the Peace Tower and the neo-Gothic Parliament Buildings rising above the office blocks of downtown Ottawa. The House of Commons was a place where he had always wanted to work, but he couldn't get a security clearance. Instead, Hamill found work at the county courthouse and a seniors' home. The judges, lawyers and elderly people had no idea what was going on in the mind of the man who was paid to guard them. When they did learn more about Bruce Hamill, the people who had known him during his short career as a security guard would shudder with dread.

The Ottawa train station is not a busy place, so it didn't take Hamill long to buy a ticket to Brockville. He had no baggage. He carried a pipe wrench that he had wrapped in newspapers and put into two shopping bags. With a bit of a limp, he walked through the sliding doors of the station to the waiting train, a milk-run that stopped at the towns of the Ottawa Valley, the villages along the St. Lawrence River, and the small cities on the north shore of Lake Ontario before reaching Toronto five hours later. By late morning, he was travelling through the fields and woods of the flat land that lies between Ottawa and the St. Lawrence, through little Ottawa Valley towns with names like Kemptville and Smith's Falls. He spent the hour of the trip trying to keep straight everything Mike had told him. Any deviation in the plan would cause it to fail. It wasn't just the outcome of the plan that was important. It was the ritual that mattered. If the timing was wrong, all of this would be for nothing.

As the train rolled through the countryside, which was still lush from the spring's heavy rains, Hamill thought about the problems he was having at home. His Philippines-born wife had begun to rebel over the visits to Brockville, and, rightly, suspected Hamill was seeing a male lover. The Hamills had a baby girl that was adding strain to a marriage that was already explosive. The rage that had caused Hamill so much trouble in his life was building again. The fights were becoming more vicious. In recent weeks, Hamill stopped talking, at least to his wife. Now his inner thoughts were becoming more bizarre, and Mike was shaping and directing them.

Hamill had been seeing Mike Krueger since 1989, but this visit was to be special: Krueger's first day pass off the grounds of a psychiatric hospital in thirty-five years. The Brockville hospital's staff thought Hamill and Krueger were going downtown to the Dairy Queen and for a walk along the St. Lawrence River. Then they were supposed to go to a Swiss Chalet. They would buy a pizza to take back to the hospital and spend the evening together. They, however, had other plans.

From the Brockville train station, Hamill limped down the main street until he found the town's Canadian Tire store. Its staff thought he looked weird as he lugged his heavy wad of newspaper through the air-conditioned aisles of the store. He stopped at the counter where guns and hunting knives were sold and spent more than an hour with a bored clerk, examining every blade, looking for just the right one. Then, taking much less time, he found a cheap hatchet and a sleeping bag.

"How will you be paying for that?" the store clerk asked as Hamill dropped his purchases on the counter with a clunk.

Hamill handed the woman a MasterCard. He stayed silent as she put it through the scanner. The card was valid. Hamill signed the paper that the clerk put in front of him while the woman stuffed everything into a big plastic bag.

"Can I put that in, too?" she asked, pointing at the newspaper-swaddled wrench.

"Sure," Hamill said.

The next stop was the town's drug store, where Hamill bought a pack of Nytol, a brand of over-the-counter sleeping pill. Then, after lugging his bag of weapons for about twenty minutes in the building heat, he stopped in a grove of trees, pulled everything out of the Canadian Tire bag and repacked the knife, hatchet and pipe wrench inside the sleeping bag. Ten minutes later, shortly after two in the afternoon, he was at the Brockville Psychiatric Hospital. He walked up to the receptionist at the front door, dropped the sleeping bag with its cargo of weapons on her counter, and told her he had arrived to escort Mike Krueger on a walk on the grounds.

A few minutes later, Krueger arrived from K-ward on the second floor of the hospital. He was dressed in a checkered shirt and a pair of jeans, his thinning hair cropped into a brush cut. Krueger is a short man with bandy legs and a pot belly. His face is forgettable, with small, piggy eyes, an average-sized nose, and poor bone structure. In proportion to his small body, his head seems over-large. Krueger's hand's are small, like those of a ten-year-old boy's. His skin is pale. Usually, he has bad breath, and he squints because of his lousy eyesight. He's also hard of hearing, although his deafness is rather selective.

Hamill signed Krueger out on what would be the first of two day passes. This one was for the hospital grounds only. The Brockville institution has a large tract of land. Part of the grounds are lawns and gardens, but the acres of woods held more attractions for busy homosexuals like Krueger and Hamill, who had dubbed the forested part of the hospital lands "Procreation Park". In the weeks before this visit, they had picked out a special place in a sumach grove. Lugging the sleeping bag and its lethal contents, they headed for the shrubs. Within a few minutes, they had hidden the weapons along the trail through the bushes. On the way back to the hospital, they ran into Krueger's fellow patient, Dennis Kerr. He was just the man they were looking for.

Dennis was a skinny young man, somewhat younger-looking than his twenty-seven years, who was something of a jailhouse lawyer and a musician of moderate skill. Dennis believed Krueger had inherited a lot of money, and Kerr was supposed to borrow five hundred dollars to buy a set of used drums from a music store in Kingston. Krueger had spelled out exactly what the payments were to be, the rate of interest, and the collateral.

Kerr didn't know Krueger saw him as a "roaring street punk", a little thug who was better off dead. From Kerr's point of view, Krueger was just another horny old kiddie diddler on the hunt for men who looked like boys. Most of the other patients at Brockville felt the same way about Krueger. He was far down on the institution's social scale.

Kerr was introduced by Krueger to Hamill.

"Mr. Kerr, I'd like you to meet my good friend Bruce Hamill. Bruce, this is Dennis. In an hour, we'll be back with the money for you, Dennis. I just have to go back to my room to get it," Krueger said.

Kerr began to walk away.

Turning to Hamill, Krueger said in a stage whisper, "Dennis needs some money to buy a set of drums. We'll just give it to him, then we'll go into town."

Hamill flushed and Krueger chortled. They hurried back into the hospital, filled out the papers for the second escorted pass, this time lasting three hours. Hamill folded Krueger's day pass slip and stuck it in his pocket. Instead of heading into the town, they made their way to sumach grove, knowing that Kerr would soon be there to meet them.

Kerr arrived on time, not knowing that the bushes around him were salted with weapons. Hamill stood among the trees, but Krueger lay hidden in the bushes. As Kerr opened his mouth to ask where Krueger and the money was, he heard a slight yelp. Krueger, reaching for the pipe wrench, had sliced his finger on a pull tab from a pop can. Undeterred, Krueger raised the wrench and slammed it down on Kerr's head. Kerr turned to Krueger, cried out, "what did you do that for?" and slumped down, dying.

"I could barely lift the thing, let alone swing it," Krueger said, two years later. "I did manage to do it, and I got Dennis in the head. I hit him again, after he asked his little profound question, this time from the front, and he fell down, but not without a struggle. He struggled nearly the whole time. He seemed to be afraid to die."

Hamill and Krueger fished the knife and the hatchet out of their hiding spots and began stabbing and hacking at Kerr. The attack was part murder, part dissection. The killers sexually assaulted and mutilated Kerr. Krueger poked at the body, got close to hear the death rattle, and looked carefully at the vicious wounds that he and Hamill had inflicted.

"I wanted to see if Dennis had a death rattle. They really do exist. I sat next to his body for about an hour. When he died, I heard a sound like a deep snore that came from the middle of his body. That was the death rattle. Then I saw something like a mist that came from his mouth and went up towards the sky. I know it was his spirit."

Meanwhile, Hamill began his ritual. He and Krueger, both drenched in blood, sodomised Kerr's dead body, then began to chant. When Hamill was finished, he took the pills in the Nytol pack, walked a few paces from the corpse, and lay down in the sleeping bag. Within minutes, he was asleep. Krueger kept vigil over Kerr, still poking and peering at the body. When Hamill was finally out, Krueger walked up to him, pulled the sleeping bag down to look at Hamill's nude body, then began running the blade of the knife over Hamill's chest, down his stomach, and gently over the sleeping man's testicles. Krueger thought for a moment as he caressed Hamill's body with the knife. He was tired. This was enough.

Krueger used a pair of binoculars and a white cane to find his way to a an Ontario Provincial Police station about five kilometres from the murder site. He walked up to the front counter and asked to speak with the officer in charge.

Very calmly, he spoke to Sgt. Terry Bowerman.

"I want to turn myself in. I've committed a horrible crime and I deserve to spend the rest of my life in a penitentiary," he told Bowerman.

"What have you done?" Bowerman asked Krueger. Bowerman looked over the counter at Krueger's bloody clothes.

"I killed someone. I didn't do it alone. There's another person involved. He's still there. He's a very dangerous man."

Bowerman called in Detective Sergeant Dave Bishop, a homicide expert. Bishop and two Brockville city police constables took Krueger back to the grounds of the psychiatric hospital. With Krueger squinting to see the path to the sumach grove, they set out to find Kerr's body.

It was dark and raining when they arrived. Biting insects tormented the searchers. When they approached the hospital's power house, in an area of dense bush, Krueger told them they were near the scene. Soon, they found Hamill naked, thrashing around in the trees, tormented by bugs.

"Are you here to take me?" Hamill screamed. "I'm ready. I've done everything you want. Where do I go? Is your vehicle here?" he asked.

The police ordered Hamill to lie down. Instead, he ran toward Krueger and the four officers. Crazy from the drugs, confused and covered with insect bites, Hamill flew into a psychotic rage. For several minutes, he fought with the police before they were able to handcuff him and put him in a cruiser. Krueger took the two detectives down the trail to Kerr's body. They found Kerr about 200 metres from where they had tackled Hamill.

No police officer is so hardened that he could see something like the Kerr crime scene without being sick. The body was gutted. Kerr's head had been nearly severed from his torso. The little enclave in the sumachs was sticky with the young man's blood.

"It's such a shame," Krueger said. "Such a tragedy".

The police called for help from other detachments and radioed for an ambulance. Bowerman and another officer took

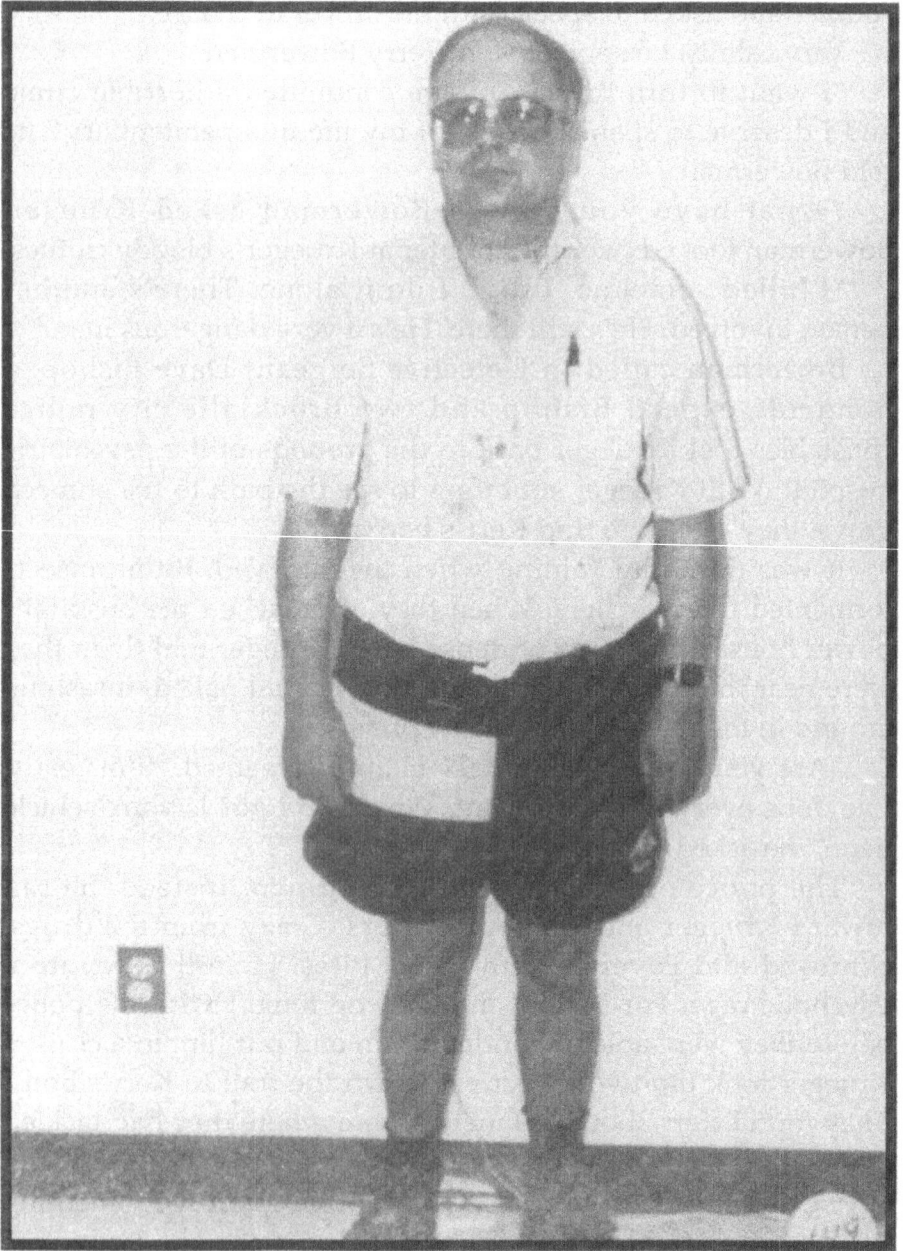

David Michael Krueger on the day he and Bruce Hamill murdered Dennis Kerr.

Photo: *Ottawa Sun*

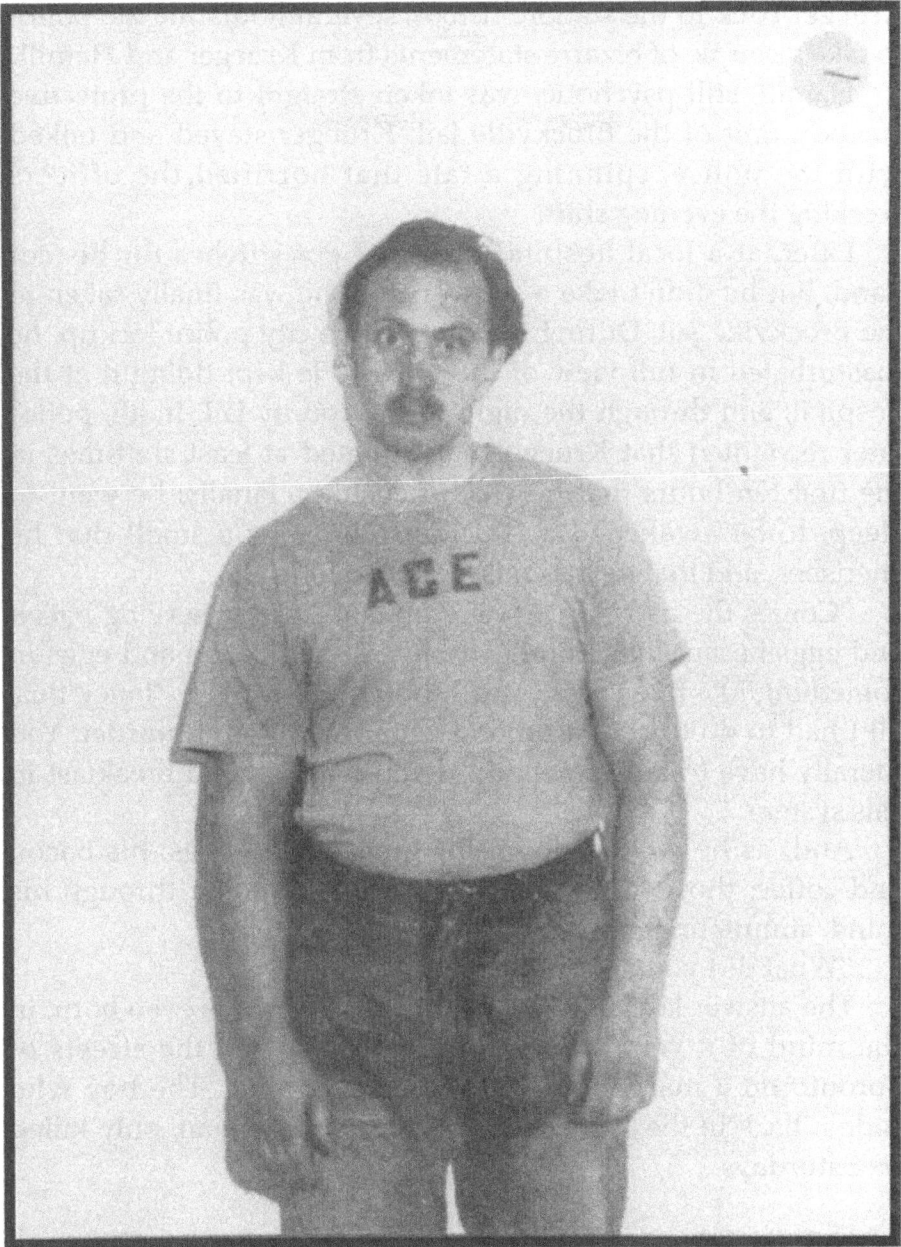

Bruce Hamill worked as a security guard at the Ottawa Court House before he committed his second murder.

Photo: *Ottawa Sun*

Krueger back to the station. It took several hours for the police to take a couple of bizarre statements from Krueger and Hamill.

Hamill, still psychotic, was taken straight to the protective custody unit of the Brockville jail. Krueger stayed and talked with the police, spinning a tale that horrified the officers working the evening shift.

Later, at a local hospital, Krueger got stitches for his cut hand, but he didn't take a shower until he was finally taken to the Brockville jail. During his time in the city police lockup, he masturbated in full view of the police. He kept doing it at the hospital, and through the night at the county jail. In all, police later recounted that Krueger masturbated at least six times in the first ten hours that he was in custody. Finally, he went to sleep, to be awakened a few hours later by a smell that he cherishes, and that he had missed for so long.

"Comes the morning, I wake up, and they're serving bacon and eggs because it's Sunday. I haven't had bacon and eggs in something like five years. And I thought to my self, 'fancy this, all I had to do to get bacon and eggs was commit murder. You literally have to kill somebody if you want a good breakfast in this system'."

And, as he wolfed down his greasy fried eggs, his bacon and coffee, those last words of Kerr's kept going through his mind, stimulating him again and again.

"What did you do that for?"

The answer lay far away, long before Kerr was even born, in the mind of a very strange boy who prowled the streets of Toronto on a marvellous red three-speed bike. The boy who rode it back in the 1950s, like the dumpy little man, only killed on Saturdays.

THE WINCHESTER HEIGHTS GANG

The seeds of the murder of Dennis Kerr were sown in the months before the beginning of World War II. In a ward of a Toronto hospital, a strange, fussing baby was born out of wedlock. Childrens' Aid Society social workers were waiting in a corner of the delivery room to begin the task of disposing of it.

The baby was Peter Woodcock, who, in the fullness of time, would deliberately and carefully re-create himself as David Michael Krueger, serial killer.

Hospital records show Peter Woodcock was born 5 March, 1939, in Toronto. Depending on which forms you read, Woodcock's mother was either a seventeen-year-old factory worker or a nineteen-year-old prostitute. Either way, she was supposed to have been active and attractive. His father was alleged to be a nineteen-year-old soldier. The records make it appear that World War II brought them together, but a little math shows Wanita Woodcock got pregnant in 1938. The war didn't start until her baby was six months old. Four years later, Wanita gave birth to another illegitimate child, a girl this time. She was adopted and had a normal life, and, as far as anyone knows, has never gone looking for her long-lost brother.

Apparently, there was nothing unusual about Wanita's pregnancy or Peter's birth. The Children's Aid social workers who supervised the baby's entry into the world allowed his mother to keep him for a month and breast feed him. Even in those first days of his life, he was described as a "feeding problem" and he cried constantly. When his mother finally gave Peter up, he was sent from one foster home to the next because Childrens' Aid didn't want any of the foster parents to bond with him. Day after day, he did nothing but cry. He never slept. He never ate. The troubling behaviour lasted all of that first year. The various foster parents tried different diets to try to get the baby to gain weight, but nothing worked and he became more bizarre and unwanted.

After Peter's first birthday, he was terrified of anyone who came near him. He learned to talk when he was approaching two years, but the speech was incoherent. It wasn't ordinary baby talk. People described it as strange whining noises. And it seems the weirdness was not just Peter's. Some of the foster families were uncaring, cold and brutal. Since the foster families weren't allowed to adopt him or even get to know him well, they basically looked after Peter for the money that Childrens' Aid paid them. Once, the baby was brought into a hospital emergency ward with a twisted neck, the result of a beating by one of the foster parents. It seems that even more nasty tortures were being done to the child. His clinical file is much too silent about this period in his life, but Krueger's memory is credible:

"When I was put up for adoption, I was bounced around from place to place. I was ignored for long periods of time, left to lie in darkness. Hardly anyone every picked me up, held me or things like that. This happened in foster homes and other institutions. There was no attempt at bonding," he says.

Finally, when he was three years old, he was sent to his last foster home. Frank and Susan Maynard were an upper-middle-class couple with a son of their own who lived in one of the better sections of what was then northern Toronto, the Yonge Street-Lawrence Avenue area. Throughout the war, the Maynards had taken in orphaned and poor children until permanent homes were found for them. Why they ended up hanging on to Woodcock is a mystery. Likely, they just felt sorry for him.

There was room in the Maynards' spacious home for one more child. The house is gone now and a church stands on the site, but pictures of the place show that it was one of those ample, three-storey Edwardian homes built on a shady, quiet street. Frank Maynard was an accountant who seems to have fit well with the image of the stereotypical father of the 1940s and 1950s. His son, George, was ten years older than the little boy who had come to live with him. George and Peter were never very close. George saw Peter as just one of a string of kids passing through, and by the time the Maynards decided to keep Peter, George was a teenager. When the killings started, George was university student. He went on to become a successful lawyer.

In some ways, Peter settled into the household quickly, growing very conscious of his new middle-class standing. In fact, his sense of class snobbery developed faster than most of his other social instincts. He looked down on the poorer people of Toronto, families like the ones he had stayed with in foster homes. There's no record of Woodcock harming kids in parts of the city like his own. He always committed his crimes in the poorer neighbourhoods.

Most of his views on class seem to have come from his new foster mother, Susan Maynard. She was a plump, short woman from a wealthy Maryland background. Susan comes across as a tyrant in most conversations with Krueger, and there's no doubt that she was forceful, with an overly-developed sense of what was proper. Still, she must have had a tremendous amount of charity, strength and patience to deal with the baby that she had taken into her home. In all of the records kept on the family, there was never a suggestion that she wanted to give her weird child back, and she had many chances. She also had many reasons. Peter still screamed any time a stranger approached and he looked like a child with rickets. For Susan, raising Peter was a full-time job. He never let go of her. She became attached to Peter and defensive, insisting to sceptical doctors and friends that her damaged little toddler was improving.

"I have several earliest memories," Krueger says. "One is being carried by my foster mother, backwards and forwards across the living room. I was around three years of age. The radio was playing. Probably it was classical music. It was in music that I defined my emotions as a child because it could be joyous or sad."

Next door, there had been a vacant lot, and Frank Maynard used it in the winter as a place to build a skating rink for the two boys.

Peter wished they had stayed in that house, but when he was ten, they moved to Lytton Boulevard, to the place which later became notorious for a few months as the home of Peter Woodcock, child killer. It was a spacious house, with a large sunroom and an attached garage. The Maynards and their foster son settled into a comfortable, substantial home that had antique gaslights that still worked.

Gradually, people began agreeing with Susan that Peter seemed to be getting better, at least physically. He had stopped screaming around strangers. At the same time, by the age of seven, he was already developing the pool of knowledge that he draws on for his fantasy world. He needed to do something to fill his time. Other kids thought he was strange and wouldn't play with him. He was a natural target for bullies. That, in more than half a century, would never change, and his resentment would be the fuel that fed his cruel inner world.

For five years, starting at the age of seven, Woodcock was treated for his behaviour problems by doctors at the Hospital for Sick Children. The entire family needed help coping. The Maynards were well into middle age and the strain of looking after this strange ward was showing. Susan Maynard's life stopped being centred on her own son and her husband, and now revolved around her damaged foster son. Her time was organized around their frequent trips to the hospital.

When they weren't downtown seeing specialists, the mother and boy were home at their comfortable house, with its overstuffed furniture, its knickknacks and mementos. On a mantle, there was a set of Indian War-vintage army knives Susan brought with her from her childhood home. Krueger remembers the snow falling outside the house's bay windows, the blinking Christmas lights, Susan coming in to light the gaslight in his room. She warned him never to turn the gaslight off, only down, so that gas fumes couldn't leak. There was a little electric light over his bed so he could read, and Krueger used it every night.

During the day, he indulged his fetishes for city travel and public transportation.

"Toronto back in the forties and fifties was an exciting place to grow up," he said one winter day in Penetanguishene, when the roads to the isolated institution where he is being kept were barely passable. "I went to the Santa Claus Parade in 1946 or 1947 and watched it go down University Avenue. When it was over, we walked to Yonge Street, where there was an even more fantastic parade: all these streetcars, which had been made to wait at the intersections until the parade was over. I was fascinated. They were so exotic. I spent about an hour on Yonge Street with Mother and watched all the streetcars on the side streets until they vanished, and there were just the Yonge cars running up and down.

"I remember my first sight of the Yonge Street streetcars, great big monsters. Everything seemed bigger, those red and green streetcars running up and down on their tracks, one right after the other, all filled with people. I used to sneak on them, and the drivers soon got to know me. I would go all the way down to Queen, then take another streetcar that looked similar but a little different, and head on out to see where it went. When it got to the end of its line, I would take another streetcar. One time I got lost, at the age of four, and ended up in Port Credit, watching the Credit River flow by. Just to the north were empty fields. So I invested a nickel and called home.

"It was then I had my first encounter with the police, a couple of nice, friendly men dressed in blue."

The Maynards took these travels seriously and tried to get the staff at the Hospital for Sick Children to do something about the boy's wandering. And all of his trips away from home were not nearly so romantic or carefree. Several nights, he never came home, and one time his parents searched all evening and found him cowering under bushes. He said he was hiding from other children and that he wanted to stay out where God could protect him.

Strange things began happening inside the house, too.

One day, Susan left the house for twenty minutes and came back to find her canary dead. Peter had laid it out on the piano, surrounded by candles. He told his mother that the family dog had killed the bird. She was mortified by the murder of the canary and scared that Peter would burn the house down. Other times when he was left alone, he tore down the window blinds, chopped up all of his socks, carved symbols into the dining room table and smashed a radio. He liked to sit alone and cut his clothing.

Of course, to David Michael Krueger, the strange behaviour was someone else's fault:

"After I was six, seven or eight, Mother hit me with a beaded rod. Mother underwent a marked change in her personality. Something mysteriously happened. They were in New York, and my brother, who was ten years older than me and so was a teenager, was looking after me. He was out with his friends and had left me alone. I went all across the city, going on all of the streetcar routes. When Mother came home, she was brought into the house on a stretcher. In whispers, they told me mother was pushed down the stairs in Grand Central Station by a drunk who tried to get her purse. She came home with a concussion. We had to be very quiet, very considerate.

"She was allowed to do whatever she wanted, yell scream or cry at us, but we were not allowed to answer back. My brother started doing the normal teenage thing, staying out. Then the beatings started for me.

"There were good times, too. I remember on my ninth birthday, she took me aside at the celebration and said 'You're nine years of age. When you're outside, you represent the family. When people see you, they will judge the rest of us by how you behave. So be on your best behaviour. Remember, we trust you'."

That last story doesn't fit with the psychiatric record. In fact, anything good that he says about his childhood should be taken with a healthy ration of cynicism. Nothing in his files suggests he was anything but a weird little kid looking at the world through pop-bottle-bottom glasses. Whether he was a trusted ambassador of the affluent Maynard family or not, Woodcock was on the move. He started tracing all the streetcar lines on maps that he kept in his bedroom, exploring neighbourhoods, climbing through ravines. There was only one place he wouldn't go: Regent Park, which was then Toronto's toughest neighbourhood.

When he wasn't physically wandering around the city, he was travelling mentally. At school, he chewed pencils and stared out the window. He created fantasy worlds where he was the all-powerful leader.

"It was safer being by myself. I got picked on because I was smaller, unco-ordinated. I used to walk crab-like. Even as a teenager, in the Sea Cadets, I would find myself walking with my right arm and right leg coming out together."

Lots of bright, awkward kids are picked on and labelled "nerds" by their school mates. Only rarely do they become killers. The Maynards and the Childrens' Aid Society knew Peter had problems. They tried to shelter him from other kids, but the only thing that could have worked would have been a decision to pull him out of school and teach him at home. Instead, the Maynards cast around eastern North America, looking for an institution where Peter would be safe.

The first private school that Woodcock was sent to was near the Maynard home. Waycroft School had a very small student body, but there were still enough kids to cause Peter trouble. He wouldn't play games or make friends. Sometimes, he came home very disturbed, and he had a couple of bouts of twitching that each lasted two weeks. It was obvious he needed more help than any regular school could give.

As Woodcock became more strange, his foster mother became more protective.

One day, as she sat in a small, grim office at the Hospital for Sick Children, she turned to Dr. Hawke, a psychologist, and said, "I think Peter would do better if we legally adopted him."

Hawke looked at her, turning a greenish shade of white, and said, "for God's sake woman, don't do that. You don't know what the future holds."

Susan Maynard did give up on the idea of adopting Peter, but she kept looking for a place to send him. Even though he was still a ward of Childrens' Aid, she was willing to pay whatever the best institutions charged. The better places, in the United States, were full, so she haunted the schools for disturbed children in Toronto, looking for one that she thought could help Peter.

"One place should have been called Stalag II. It was run by two British ex-Marines who had undergone a sex change," Krueger says. The other schools seemed no better, so Susan began travelling the province to find a place in the country that could help her boy.

In 1950, when Woodcock was eleven and Susan was busy with her search, Peter was sized up by a Children's Aid Society social worker. He was being considered for a school for disturbed children in Kingston, Ontario. Children's Aid enshrined this description in its records:

"Slight in build, neat in appearance, eyes bright, and wide open, worried facial expression, sometimes screwing up of eyes, walks brisk and erect, moves rapidly, darts ahead, interested and questioning constantly in conversation.

"Peter's main interests appear to be walking his dog, riding his bicycle and attending the Salvation Army meetings. At the Exhibition, he wanted most to see the Canadian Armed Services in Action— interested in planes, tanks and anti-aircraft equipment. He attributes his wandering to feeling so nervous that he just has to get away. In some ways, Peter has little capacity for self-control. He appears to act out almost everything he thinks and demonstrates excessive affection for his foster mother. Although he verbalizes his resentment for other children, he has never been known to physically attack another child. He becomes angry with adults, especially when he feels misunderstood. He seems to handle his fears by avoiding — for example, staying inside when there are other children on the street ...

"He kisses the mother two or three times on each departure ...

"Peter apparently has no friends. He plays occasionally with younger children, managing the play. When with children his own age, he is boastful and expresses determinedly ideas which are unacceptable and misunderstood. Recently, Peter was to be included in a Club on the street to raise money for the Red Cross. He wanted to have a Dog and Cat Club and when turned down, he told the boys he liked animals a lot better than boys, thereby immediately losing his place in the club."

The boy, only eleven years old, was already sending out danger signals. When a Childrens' Aid social worker who was helping with the assessment walked with him through the crowded Canadian National Exhibition grounds on an August day, Peter turned to him and said, "I wish a bomb would fall on the Exhibition and kill all the children."

The Children's Aid Society sent him to Sunnyside Children's Centre in Kingston. The fearful, thin but somewhat friendly child fit into the routine of this special school for disturbed children, the same way he fits in with the inmates of the hospital for the criminally insane today. He preferred reading to any kind of physical activity. When adults weren't around, he played sexual games with the other kids. At summer camp in 1952, he spent his time in the wilderness walking around with armloads of books. When counsellors found him lying on the side of the road, he told them that he just wanted to see how the underside of cars looked. On quiet days, he sat on a curb with a watch and a Kingston bus schedule, making sure the transit system was running efficiently.

The Kingston school wanted to discharge him when he was fourteen, which was the normal age for release, but social workers thought he was not ready to be on the loose again in Toronto. He talked too much about The Winchester Heights Gang, an imaginary group of boys that Woodcock led on adventures. In real life, he was caught fondling an eleven-year-old girl.

Even then, two years before the first rapes and murders, Woodcock knew that his sex drive was stronger and more dangerous than most childrens:

"I did have a hyper sex drive. It was too strong, really. The closest I ever came to having normal sex with a consenting female was when I was thirteen. She was twelve. She was the queen bee of the orphanage. We both wondered what it was like. Grown ups did it. The animals, birds, fishes, they all did it, so why not us? We watched and we waited. We both agreed that we would do it and we both solemnly swore a blood oath that we would go all the way together. It's funny looking back on it, but at the time it was so cute. There was a terrible embarrassment and also a terrible joy.

"We waited until we knew the superintendent had gone to a fundraiser and the staff was busy with all of the other kids, who we had bribed to keep the staff occupied. We snuck into the superintendent's office and turned the lights out. She was totally in the altogether, as was I, admiring what each other had. We felt, we touched, we did all the other things. Feelings were getting more and more urgent. I was lying on my back. I was on fire, like in that country song *I'm on Fire with Desire for Elvira*, and she's lowering herself onto me, with her back to me. When the lips of her vagina touched the outer skin of the penis, it was just so wild. I wanted to knock her hands out. We were half way to inserting it, and who should come in but Miss Townshend, the Superintendent.

"She lectured us for about two hours solid, then other members of the staff came in and spelled her off. She scolded, she threatened, she complained. The one threat that really terrified me was that she would call my mother if this ever happened again. To me, this was the ultimate disaster.

"That was my first and only, and my last. I learned an unfortunate lesson, that I couldn't trust any grownup. My mother had caught me exploring myself twice, once when I was alone, in bed, when I was six. That's the normal behaviour of five or six year olds, but Mother didn't think so. The other time was at the age of seven, when a girl wanted to find out why she was different from me and quite frankly, I enjoyed her explorations, and I explored her. The Warden (his mother) caught us once again. With my family, you didn't talk about sex. In our house, mentioning any part of the body was completely forbidden."

The years in Sunnyside were the best times of his life, he says. He missed Toronto, but he wasn't picked on by other kids at the Kingston public school that he went to. The new horn-rimmed glasses that he was fitted out with when he was fourteen made him look even more gawky, but he still fit in much more easily with the Sunnyside kids. The staff trusted him to go on his bicycle, and it was in Kingston that his fetish for transit punctuality reached full bloom. Woodcock shared a bedroom in an old mansion with three other children. He's been back, as a supervised student taking Queen's University night courses, to see Sunnyside and the school that he went to.

"One time, when I was in Sea Cadets, I was posted on guard duty, Lee Enfield rifle, great coat and all. I had the regular Navy stove hat. There I was, standing guard on this National Defence property in Kingston. I had been told the corp was having a party. I volunteered to secure the perimeter because I'm not that much of a party goer. So there I was with the belt and the ammo. The rifle was loaded, it had to be, the bayonet was stuck in. There I was, fourteen, feeling I'm a real man, finally. The officer of the day said 'You have to stay there until you are relieved'. That was really simple and straightforward. In the Navy, you don't desert your post. So the party breaks up about midnight and everyone goes home. The corporal of the guard makes the rounds and picks up everyone, but they forget about me. So I stayed there."

Staff at the Childrens Centre had called the commanding officer of the Sea Cadets, looking for Woodcock, then called the police. Someone on the police department suggested checking the camp.

"About 6:30 in the morning, a Kingston police cruiser quietly comes up with its lights out. When they turned them on, they were confronted by a Sea Cadet, fourteen years of age, with a bayonet on the end of the rifle, fully loaded, with the safety off, and 'Identify Yourselves' coming from him."

Despite the progress that Woodcock had made, nearly everyone involved knew that returning Woodcock to the Maynard home in September, 1954, was a mistake. He was sent back to Waycroft, where he tried to fit in by joining the glee club and the drama club. Everything seemed to end in embarrassment:

"When I was a very young youngster, I could imitate most animal sounds. I loved to sing, and at this private school they put me into, Waycroft, Sasschenhaussen II, they were running an auditorium once a year. The kids would put on a little play, and because I could do all kinds of sounds, I was in demand as a back-up person. I would sit in the wings and croak like a frog. Not that 'ribbit, ribbit' sound, either. I could chirp and croak, make that churling sound. I could make a very convincing bark of several breeds, and my whinnies were so good that you would think a horse was there. And that was one of my proudest things. And I loved to be trusted, that was one of the things I wanted most, to be trusted and approved of.

"One night in the spring (of 1955), I was swinging away on one of the swings by the Don River, which runs behind this old school, and my voice cracked. I couldn't do any sounds after that, and the performance was only two nights away. I went through agony and anxiety because I was afraid that I was letting everyone down. It was a painful moment, but it was also humourous, I suppose."

After a year at Waycroft, he went to Lawrence Park Collegiate, where kids who recognised him from public school started picking on him again. Six weeks after the school year began, he wanted out. Some of the students pushed him down an embankment and broke his bike. They ripped the Sea Cadet badges that he had earned in Sunnyside off his jacket. Three days later, he started at Bloordale College School, a small private institution, as a Grade 9 student. He stayed there until Grade 11, "when the police mercifully put an end to my education and my career". He would come home from school shaken and disturbed. In the evenings, he spent time alone, with a book or a radio, said his prayers and went to bed.

In the early years of high school, he had excelled in Science, History and English, often getting 100 per cent on tests. When he wrote a negative critique of Shaw's Pygmalion in Grade 9, his teacher said "Maybe you're just too smart". He answered, in his fawning, clumsily diplomatic way, "No. There's so much more you can teach me. "

Some adults liked the boy because of his quick wit and his knowledge. He could hold his own in any conversations. Like most other psychopaths, he has always been charming and manipulative. He used those skills on children, too.

A new, wonderful white and red three-speed bicycle was evolving into the centrepiece of Peter's fantasy world. He led the Winchester Heights Gang of five hundred invisible but obedient boys as he peddled for miles across Toronto and the farmland north of the city.

"When I was living at home, especially in my teenage years, I rode my bike everywhere. You can go places on a bicycle that people on foot would need a long time to get into. I wore glasses, but I could see out of the back of my head. I would often speed down pathways that other people who were chasing me couldn't handle. They would flip over their handlebars and fall ass-over-tea kettle. I would do, on Saturdays and Sundays, anywhere from fifty to sixty miles a day on my bike. It wouldn't be a straight line, it would be all over the city. As a result, I got to know Toronto really good.

"Just because there was snow around in the winter, why put the bike away? Snow and ice made riding more fun. He says he never dumped it. He would ride west down Eglinton Avenue from Yonge Street, go on the Humber River when it was frozen and ride along the river all the way to Queen Street. Some of the winters in the mid-'50s, there was very little snow in Toronto, but it was so cold that all of the rivers froze over.

"I would go tearing down the Humber River, often doing forty miles an hour, with people hollering, 'Hey, kid, you're going to lay her down'. I would ride along the lake, just outside the breakwall all the way through to the Western Gap and come back in on Parliament Street. I would make that trip in half an hour, from Eglinton to the Humber, or sometimes I would just take off up the Don River."

When he was riding at night in the Riverdale area, which in those days was a tough part of Toronto, he would switch off his light and ride up the frozen Don River so that no one would rob him of his bike. Sometimes other kids would lurk behind him on their bikes, but bigger boys who chased Woodcock risked falling through the ice, since virtually every kid his age was much bigger and heavier.

When he wasn't riding, he was stopping adults on the street to ask questions and getting to know every streetcar conductor in the city. At home, he watched the Mickey Mouse Club and fantasized that the Winchester Heights gang was doing some of the same things that Mickey's friends did. But he had no friends his own age, only the TV, the radio, and his classical music records. He turned his nose up at Elvis Presley and the new rock and roll songs that were being played on CHUM, the local teen station. That summer, he got a job parking cars at Casa Loma, a giant mansion that is one of Toronto's busier tourist attractions. It was the only job that he ever had outside of an institution. His boss was happy with his work, and he kept working weekends after the 1956-1957 school year started. The Maynard family and their foster child settled into a seemingly normal routine. No one except Peter knew what he was doing on those long bicycle trips. His parents knew about The Winchester Heights Gang and the fascination with the transit system, but that all seemed harmless. They didn't know about Woodcock's dreams and his new interest in human anatomy.

* * *

The awful dreams of murder and rape started in February, 1956.

At the same time, a new, "alien" self seemed to enter Woodcock's body. That was the way he saw the strong attraction that he was developing for small children and the vicious fantasies he had, day and night, about killing them. Every time he saw a child, he wondered what its private parts looked like. When he led the invisible Winchester Heights gang, they went on much more evil missions.

Woodcock began acting on his new urges by playing sex games with small children, bribing them with rides on his wonderful bike. At first, there was no violence:

"I was afraid of blood. There were so many people who were willing to come with me that I felt, 'why should I have bothered going on to the next phase'."

Simply conning a child into stripping naked was enough, at first, but Woodcock had urges to do more. Sex wasn't his motivation. It was rage. Like many other serial killers, Krueger was unable to perform sexual intercourse in any normal sense. When he embraced violence, the sexual part of his attacks were assaults on the genitals of his victims. Orgasm came later, when he fantasised about what he had done. Woodcock would have committed his first murder in the spring of 1956, but it was botched. His victim was a ten-year-old girl, a depressed child who didn't seem to care what happened to her.

"I wanted to go on to the next phase (of criminality) in March of '56. There was a ten-year-old girl. I did have plans to cut her up to see what she looked like inside. And that was the incident, plus the way that it was responded to, that laid the groundwork for the tragedies. We got lost in the ravine in the dark, and getting out seemed more important. I had a pen knife with me. When you're naive, a pen knife seems like enough to kill with.

"It was a turning point. I was already troubled with my fantasies and dreams. This ten-year-old girl, I did have plans of killing her. I didn't dawn on me that she would die. Well, I knew she would die, but that would be about the extent of it. I wanted to look at the arm, see how the muscle attaches to it. This was going to be a very thorough anatomical lesson, though I don't believe I would have been able to name a third of the things I would have seen.

"We had talked about two weeks beforehand. Cause she wanted to die. That's what gave me the idea. First, she wanted to kill herself, she actually tried a couple of times. Her father and mother were divorcing and her mother blamed her for the divorce because her dad used to climb up in bed with her and pretend she was mommy. The problems that we prattle about, parents molesting innocent children, this has been going on, I believe, down through the centuries. It was sad, so I said, 'You come with me this coming Saturday, we'll find a spot and I will kill you' and she was very grateful. She came quite willingly. When she laid down for me to cut her neck open, I had no idea how to do it, and I kept telling her, 'this is wrong'."

Nothing seemed to go right. The rendezvous was late because Woodcock had dawdled, there was only about an hour of daylight left, and he didn't want to get lost in the ravines in the dark. The stream valleys in central Toronto are a confusing series of steep hills, and this murder failed because Woodcock didn't know them as well as he thought. It took a lot longer to get to the place that Woodcock had chosen for the murder than he had expected. Woodcock and the girl looked for a better scene for the murder, then became afraid of being lost. After wandering around for three hours, they decided to climb out of the ravines and wait for another chance.

The girl's parents had become worried, and they talked to the police about Woodcock, but nothing came of the expedition until Woodcock was arrested almost a year later. The police did visit the Maynard house, setting off Woodcock's foster mother. She threatened to ground him for the rest of his life because of the scandal of having a police car parked in front of the house.

"Okay," said Woodcock, "I'll kill myself, if it will make it easier for you to hold your head up with the neighbours. If you don't want me to kill myself, I think I'll just go up to bed because I've got to go to school tomorrow."

He went up to his room. His parents followed and sat on the edge of the bed, where the fight continued. After a few minutes, Mother stormed out of the room. Woodcock's foster father stayed behind.

"Don't pick up any more children," he said quietly.

A couple of months later, after the spring floods ran through the ravines and the new leaves hid the river valleys and kids' forts, Woodcock started travelling the city on his bike. His attacks became more violent. He would choke children until they passed out, peer over their bodies, then leave them to wake up, alone and naked, in a park or ravine. Many of them never told their parents.

"I had physiology textbooks, and a lot of my offenses were anatomical explorations. I would consult a textbook an hour afterwards and say, oh, that's what that is. I was interested in everything from the top of the head to the toes, and everything in between. I never did what is considered sexual assault. There was experimentation that way. I never went out with the expectation of doing that. I would put them out and take a look, but I was also very angry. As a teenager, I was extremely angry with everyone. The rage would never really leave."

The attacks were carefully pre-planned, at least at first.

"I wouldn't go back to the area of the city where one of these encounters occurred. You never knew when you would run into one of your," Krueger couldn't find the word, which to me was obvious. "At the start of it, it was quite frankly curiosity about the difference between boys and girls and also how those difference evolved from the baby up to the grownup. There was nothing more to it than that. I found that when I was with them, we were playing around together, it was all consent because kids like to play those kind of games and the more mommy and daddy react, the more the kid gets a kick out of it. It was completely alien to my nature for the longest time to hurt anyone. Then I was watching Hitchcock and all that stuff and there was all of that violence. It was right after the war, and the war mentality stayed with us for at least fifteen years after 1945. The Lone Ranger was forever shooting guns out of people's hands, people were being banged over the head with chairs. You would see them drop, so I would often wonder 'I wonder what it would be like to hit someone over the head. Would they drop like that?' In the movies, no one ever went to the bathroom, which had me completely amazed. I was convinced when I was six or seven years old that there were two types of people in the world, those like you and me who went to the washroom and the superpeople."

In the summer, he got a job at Casa Loma as a helper in the parking lot on Saturday nights. I wondered how much Casa Loma's towers and battlements fired up Krueger's fantasy world, but it was a question that he never answered. The job left him free all day to ride his new red and green bike three-speed, with lights and reflectors on the frame. It was a solid, good quality machine suitable for forty-mile trips.

In mid-September, once school began and Woodcock had to face the misery of dealing with his peers and teachers, the attacks became deadly.

* * *

Wayne Mallette was a blonde, brown-eyed Grade 1 student who lived in the eastern Ontario village of Seeleys Bay. He, his parents, and three of his four brothers went to Toronto on Saturday, 16 September, 1956, to visit the kids' grandmother. Her home was on Empress Street, near the Canadian National Exhibition grounds.

That entire neighbourhood is gone, replaced by the Gardiner Expressway and its ramps. In 1956, it was part of southern Parkdale, on the western edge of Toronto. In late August, the neighbourhood was busy with people going back and forth to the Exhibition, but in the fall it was quiet. When the Mallettes arrived in the city, the Exhibition's roads were empty, except for popcorn boxes and candy wrappers tossed by the winds. A few guards patrolled the fair grounds, watching for kids who might try to break into the vacant buildings or climb the idle wooden Flier roller coaster.

After their four-hour trip to Toronto, the Mallette boys spent a polite amount of time with their grandmother, then began to drift away. The three older boys went downtown. Wayne stayed behind to play in the front yard. Just as it began to get dark, he disappeared.

A few minutes later, Irene began calling her son. Her husband, Jack, tried to soothe her by saying Wayne must be with his brothers. She didn't believe him, but she tried to hope. When the three older boys arrived home, Irene called the police. When they came to the door, Jack told them about Wayne's disappearance, then went with them to search.

The boy had wandered from his grandmother's yard to the main railway line that runs through the Exhibition neighbourhood. The fence along the track was hidden from the nearby houses by trees, but a path ran right along the inside edge of the chain link. It was a perfect place for boys to hide.

Somewhere near the bushes, Wayne met Peter Woodcock and his marvellous bike. Wayne told Woodcock that he had come to watch the trains. It was a subject that Woodcock could easily warm to. The boys began talking about the freights and passenger trains that were roaring by on the busy tracks. Then the conversation became more dreadful. Woodcock wanted to play.

"I took him in there and told him we could watch the trains together. Then I tried to get him to play sex games. He got scared. My alien self took over. I shoved his face down into the dirt, and he stopped breathing. I knew he was gone when I heard the death rattle," Krueger said.

In fact, the killing was more brutal. Dr. Morton Shulman, the Toronto coroner who investigated the murder, saw marks on Mallette's legs that proved he had been kicked, and found pieces of garbage stuffed into the child's mouth. Mallette had been viciously bitten on the legs. When he was found, there were still tears on his cheeks.

Woodcock had taken off all of the boy's clothes, looked at his body, then put the clothes back on.

The police search went on past midnight. A new shift of officers joined in the hunt. By 2:30 a.m., when constables Jack Smith and Robert Brown found Mallette's body, there were thirty police officers combing through the neighbourhood.

The police found Mallette fully dressed, with dirt on his underclothes. His cheeks were still pink. The hardened police officers could barely believe he was dead.

They brought Jack Mallette to the scene a few minutes later. An officer shone his flashlight on the boy's body.

"Are you sure?" the cop asked.

"I'm sure," Jack answered.

The next day, he told a news reporter, "I told Irene as gently as I could. It was the hardest thing I have done in my life."

For half an hour, the family tried to sleep. By then, Sunday morning had come. Witnesses were being brought to the Empress Street house to see if the Mallette brothers looked like a boy they had seen in the Exhibition grounds. Police investigators wanted to do more interviews with the family. The press began arriving by mid-morning.

During the first day of their investigation, the police thought the killer might be a "sex deviate", one of the flashers who had recently been frightened out of High Park during a recent police crackdown. They searched the houses that had been vacated to make way for the new expressway. There were false leads, but a few strong ones that police, at first, couldn't believe: sightings of Mallette with a youth who was not much bigger than the murdered child, a skinny kid on a flashy bike.

"An important clue in the case could be held by a boy about fifteen years of age who was seen riding his bicycle at a fast rate out of the CNE grounds by the Princes' gates. Police think he may have been riding at a full clip because he had seen something that frightened him," the *Toronto Star* reported.

The strongest hint of Woodcock's presence in the neighbourhood came from a CNE watchman who had stopped to talk to a strange-looking youth. The boy asked him, "do they ever find any bodies in the bushes?

"What would you do if you found a body in the bushes?"

"I would call the police," the guard answered.

"Aren't you a policeman?," Woodcock asked.

"No," the guard answered. The guard asked Woodcock if he had seen a body.

"No, but I saw a boy run out of the bushes. He looked just like me."

Then Woodcock got on his bicycle and rode away, back toward his home at the far end of the city.

So police had a first rate-description of Woodcock and his bike. They sent a description to every public school in the city, but not to the private school that Woodcock went to. Experts did forensic tests on Mallette's body and were even able to make a cast of the teeth imprints on the boy's legs. With the eyewitness evidence they had, police should have been able to solve the case. Instead, they sent an innocent boy to jail.

Nine days after Wayne Mallette's murder, fourteen-year-old Ronald Mowatt skipped school. That's a normal part of adolescence. So is fear of punishment. Before his parents came home, Mowatt, who seems to have been a little strange, took a blanket and a pillow, went into a crawl space under his family's veranda, and hid. He stayed there for four days.

Police joined in the search for the boy. When they found him, they moulded the boy into the murder suspect they were looking for. They even played out their scenario on the front page of the *Toronto Star*:

"Police have learned that the boy and Wayne became locked in a struggle in the bushes, the latter getting a grip on the older boy. The suspect is reported to have bitten him twice to loosen Wayne's hold, then grabbed him by the neck and held him face downward until he died of suffocation.

"He felt the boy's body go limp, knew he was dead and then became frantic.

"He pedalled away on a stolen bicycle after speaking to a CNE guard. It is reported the bicycle was found after the boy's arrest in a spot along the railway tracks near Fort York armories. He abandoned it after riding it out the gate and north to Strachan Avenue."

It was damning stuff. Of course, Mowatt's parents denied it and gave an alibi for their son. The police should have listened. Instead, within a few weeks, Mowatt was packed off to Guelph Reformatory, convicted of manslaughter.

Woodcock read all about it with considerable interest, and some anger, too. He didn't want someone else taking "credit" for one of his crimes.

There were so many clues in the Mallette murder that pointed to Woodcock. Even the front page headline in the *Toronto Star*, "Boy Murdered in CNE Grounds Seized While Watching Trains" should have set off a few alarm bells in the Maynard family, who were so well aware of Woodcock's railway fetish. Two weeks after he killed Wayne Mallette, Woodcock was given a Rorschach ink blot test by the Children's Aid Society that showed he had a large amount of cold-blooded hostility. His mother later said he should have seen a psychiatrist, but instead, she protected him "from Society". He slid in and out of his dream world, kept watch on the streetcars, and supervised the construction of an expressway that was built through the scene of his first murder.

* * *

That fall, Woodcock went out every weekend to molest children. He was working up to another killing. The teen was becoming more ferocious than most adult serial killers, barely waiting for the intense publicity of his last homicide to subside before attacking again.

Only three weeks were to pass from the time Wayne Mallette died until Woodcock killed Gary Morris, a nine-year-old boy from the what was then a grim Toronto neighbourhood, Cabbagetown. Again, Woodcock had left his upper-middle class home to kill a child from a poorer part of the city.

Woodcock had picked the scene in advance. It was Cherry Beach, a neglected piece of Toronto shoreline east of the city's docks. Woodcock met Morris at the St. Lawrence Market and talked the boy into going for a ride. One of Morris' friends saw him go and later gave a description of Woodcock to the police, but they couldn't solve this murder.

"I had known for years and years that there was a Cherry Beach. There was a huge orchard down there, I suppose, around 1812. I got hold of an old map from 1925 that showed all of the streetcar routes, and there was a Cherry Route. I began thinking that I had to follow all of those routes. I did. I started wandering around.

"Cherry Beach used to have an amusement park. I went down on a late spring day in 1955 and discovered a big swing bridge. I went over the ship channel and was impressed how wide it was. I went over the bridge, and, on the south side of the canal, saw all of these broken down factories. Then I went down to the beach. I saw all of these buildings. There had been a junction down there, and a TTC shed. I broke in and found all of these old Toronto Street Railway timetables," Krueger says, a wistful look on his face. It was more emotion than he would show for Gary Morris.

"I rode down the beach, into the sand. There was a dirt road curving out of sight. The seagulls were circling overhead, the wind was wild, sun beating down, the grass green, and so high that I couldn't see over it as I rode on my bicycle.

"I explored the beach until I was chased away by some kids."

A few weeks later, Woodcock was back at Cherry Beach, this time with a victim riding on his bike's crossbar.

"I believe he lived on Sackville. I ran into him in the St. Lawrence Market. He was wandering around, and he liked the bike.

"I was always on the prowl for someone, and since he was so interested in the bicycle, he seemed like a good catch. He was small, only nine years old.I asked if he wanted to go for a ride, and he said 'sure'. He rode on the bar, sidesaddle. I had better control of the bike that way. Cherry Beach was about a mile away. I knew Toronto well, and I had several of these parts picked out."

Krueger took him to the foot of Commissioners Street, to an empty waterfront area east of the city port. He choked the child into unconsciousness, took off his clothes, looked at the boy's body, then viciously attacked him. Barry Morris's body was found with bite marks on the neck. The boy had been beaten so hard that he died of a ruptured liver.

"It was just like all the other mistakes. This time, he died as a result of my activities. I realized it when I heard the death rattle. I went home late in the afternoon thinking, 'my God, this has got to stop'."

For a couple of days, no one believed Morris had been kidnapped. He had run away from home a couple of times, and may have been doing it again when he walked to the St. Lawrence Market. He had wanted to go to the United States to join the circus.

"There was a big stink, like the Exhibition one, but it was prolonged, because they didn't find him for a week or ten days. The tall grass is what hid him. After that, they cut it down."

"I was very frightened. I didn't want this to happen again. I didn't want them to die like that. People were getting mad. Toronto was very Victorian, but what didn't help was the circulation war that was still going on between the *Toronto Star* and the *Telegram*. If there was an accident and someone was killed, the papers would cover it with big headlines. A story about a murder became huge news."

Despite Krueger's lies to the contrary, Morris' death was no accident.

"It is a long time ago, but I still have memories of it. The memories are like a dream to me, and just about as relevant. It's like having the memories of a sixteen-year-old in the mind of a fifty-four-year-old man, but I suppose if I knew what went on in the mind of a fifty-four-year-old grandfather, I would be horrified. But, you know, you can feel what you like after the fact, but that don't change anything."

The police should have been able to match the style of this killing to the slaying of Wayne Mallette: the bite marks, the boy on the bicycle, the age of the victim. To be charitable, there was a communications problem in the police force. The downtown cops thought that the police in the boroughs were hicks and bumblers. Each force jealously guarded its information, so no one realized the pattern of Krueger's sex assaults and killings. The Toronto police were to amalgamate with departments from the suburbs on New Year's Day to form the Metro Toronto Police Department. Woodcock tried to give them their first murder to investigate: he molested and strangled a small girl in an underpass on Lakeshore Boulevard early New Year's Day. She didn't die, and was able to give the police a description of her attacker: the same boy, the same bike, the same type of assault.

Less than three weeks later, Woodcock killed again. This time, the police couldn't miss, no matter how inept they were.

* * *

On Saturday, 19 January, 1957, Woodcock got up early and did a few chores around the house. He listened to some music, had lunch, walked to a few stores on Yonge Street, and enjoyed the soft air of a mid-winter thaw that began to melt the thin layer of snow that had blanketed the city since Christmas. He went home, wheeled his bike from the porch, and coasted down Yonge Street, past the small stores at Eglinton Ave., the CHUM building at St. Clair, where disc jockeys were gearing up for the Elvis Presley tour that was starting soon, and down to the Bloor intersection. Woodcock turned left, rode for a while, and stopped at the Danforth Radio Store. Diane Coates, a thirteen-year-old school girl, later told the police that she remembered seeing him in there, and that she had noticed him the summer before in the Jane and Bloor Street areas. There was nothing unusual about Woodcock going into a radio store. In fact, nothing seemed strange that day to anyone who knew him. He was home in time for dinner. After he ate, he went to work at Casa Loma. The next day, Woodcock was too tired to go to church, so he stayed home and watched television. Everything seemed normal. At 3:30 that Saturday afternoon, Carole Voyce had been playing with her friend Johnny Auld in front of Johnny's apartment house on Danforth Avenue while their mothers visited inside. Woodcock rode up to them on that fabulous bicycle. He was wearing a dark windbreaker and blue slacks. His hair was slicked back and he looked at the children through horn-rimmed glasses.

"How old are you?" Woodcock asked the little girl, who had long brown hair, a pretty round face, and who stood only three feet high.

"Four," she replied.

"And how old are you?" he asked Johnny.

"Four," the boy replied.

"How do you like my bicycle?"

"I think it's swell," Johnny said.

"Have you ever been to East York?" Woodcock asked the children.

"No," they answered.

"Have you ever been to the lake?".

This time, the children answered "yes".

"Would you like to go for a ride on my bicycle?"

"Yes," they both said, and the children walked toward the shiny machine and the pimply-faced boy.

"I think I'll take you," he said, pointing at Johnny. Then he paused. "No," he said. "I'll take you," and turned to Carol.

Then he took her hand and began walking down Danforth Ave., toward the ravines. He balanced the bike with his other hand. Two minutes later, a woman saw Woodcock riding his bicycle along the slushy street, with the girl balanced on the handlebars. She wore a grey snow suit, red mittens and black boots.

A few minutes later, Carole's mother came out of the Auld apartment began looking for her.

"Where's Carole?" she asked.

"She's gone for a bike ride with a high school boy," Johnny Auld replied.

The frantic mother called the police, and within ten minutes, two cops, Alex Busby and Earl Snider, arrived at the Auld's apartment. Ray Voyce got into the car and began cruising the area, while a description of the missing girl was broadcast to police officers across Toronto.

Within ninety minutes of the kidnapping, off-duty officers from nearby police divisions were being called in. A search party was organized shortly after dark. TV stations interrupted their programs to broadcast pictures of Carole and to ask for clues. Sixty police officers searched the area where Woodcock took the girl. Police planned to call in five hundred civil defense volunteers, but they weren't needed. The search for Carole Voyce had ended with the three revolver shots that echoed through the Rosedale ravine, below Toronto's wealthiest neighbourhood. Constable Ernie Booth found her frozen and mutilated body near the Bloor Viaduct at 11:09 p.m.. His shots signalled the end of a missing person search and the beginning of a manhunt.

Carole's father had searched all evening and was back in a local police station when the police constables at the ravine called in that they had found his girl's body.

They drove the shattered man to the crime scene, where he had to share the pain that Jack Mallette had endured in the trees by the lakeshore railway tracks. The coroner and forensic experts were averting their eyes and piecing together the crime that had occurred only a few hours before.

Woodcock had taken the girl to a ravine near Auld's house. He talked her into going down the hillside. When she wasn't looking, he had slipped his arm around her neck and choked her until she passed out. Then he jammed his fingers into her eyes. He took off her clothes and examined her body, the way he had peered at the bodies of a hundred other unconscious children. As she choked, she ripped her fingernails on Woodcock's clothes and tore at the mud with her hands. Woodcock stuck his fingers in her vagina, then thrust a stick into her body. This was the blow that killed her.

Carole's murderer looked around the ravine and became terrified that he was about to be caught. He tried to push his bike up the steep, wet clay bank, back to the road above. When he slipped back down to the murder scene, he went back to Carole Voyce's body and kicked her in the head. Woodcock went into the woods, circled around, and came back to look at the child's body. Then he wheeled his bike to a pathway that led back to the road. Fred Callum, a railway yard worker, saw Woodcock come up out of the ravine and get on his bike. Other people saw Woodcock, too: a University of Toronto professor who was stopped by the wild-eyed youngster and told: "If there's a murder down there, they'll try to blame it on me." A school mate of Woodcock's saw him walk by. He wasn't hard to miss: few kids rode their bikes in January in the Toronto of the 1950s.

For the next three days, police cars patrolled the street in front of Johnny Auld's house in case the killer tried to hurt their best witness. The newspapers ran huge headlines, and on the front page of the *Toronto Star* was a handwritten note from Raymond Voyce that read:

"To the sick man who did this terrible thing to my little girl.

Give yourself up before it happens again."

Toronto Telegram reporter Doug Creighton, in the paper's main front-page story, called Woodcock a "pimply faced sex maniac" and said police were "personally aroused by a murder vicious beyond description."

It was the first big test for the city's new Metro force. More than 2,300 police officers in the Toronto area questioned every teenager who resembled a composite drawing made from the description that Johnny Auld and the other witnesses gave them. Cops who were off-duty were called in to help. Teens were stopped as they walked down the street and were questioned in the park. The day after the murder, one boy tried to run away when police stopped him near the Canadian National Exhibition grounds. Dozens of cops swept through the area, so close to the scene of Woodcock's first murder. When they caught the teen, they realized he wasn't the murderer. Another boy matching Woodcock's description was grilled for four hours that Sunday afternoon, until police found a witness who saw him in a record store at the time of the murder. Another youth, a Hamilton, Ontario, university student, was arrested on a train because he looked like the boy in the composite drawing.

The drawing was bang on. Yet, the boy the police searched for was already in their office. Woodcock, always a welcome visitor at the station near his house, stopped in to see the police the day after the killing.

"If you're going to do something, the last thing you do is break the patterns that you've set," he told said forty years later, playing the master criminal and, at the same time, underscoring the fact that he was stone crazy by the time he killed Carole Voyce.

"Keep normal routines. It's only common sense that, if you're up to something, you don't draw attention to yourself. After all, the perfect crime is the one that hasn't happened yet, or, at least, that they don't know about. The guy who switched the Mona Lisa in the Louvre had an exact copy. If there is no reason to suspect that someone's switched it, then no one is going to investigate. If I had switched it and sold it to some collector, the last thing I would do is go out on a buying spree. For me to have stepped out of character by not going into the police station would have been a grave mistake. They expected me to come in on a regular basis, just because I was one of those kids who came in on a regular basis. You don't do anything to arouse suspicion."

Copycat criminals used the murder to frighten other victims. On Euclid Street, a youth raped a woman at gunpoint and told her he was Voyce's killer. The woman, who had given birth only a couple of weeks before, answered her apartment door and found the gun, which was probably a toy, stuck in her face. Another boy said the same thing when he tried to rob a woman in the countryside north of Toronto.

Already, police had made the connection between Gary Morris' murder at Cherry Beach and the killing of Carole Voyce. A $5,000 reward was posted. The new Metro Toronto police force finally had its first murder, courtesy of Peter Woodcock, and it had the city on edge.

Constable Jean Newman, a mother of two, went on TV to beg the parents of the murderer to turn in their son and to promise that he would be given a mental examination. Carole Voyce's father wrote a note that was published on the front page of the *Toronto Telegram*: "To the sick man who did this terrible thing to my little girl. Give yourself up before it happens again."

On the Monday morning that Woodcock was arrested, his brother, then a law student at Osgoode Hall, sat reading the *Telegram* in the Maynard family's living room. He looked at the composite, then looked at Peter.

"What have you been doing these days?" he asked jokingly.

"Nothing," said the killer, as he headed out the door to school. Two days after the murder, these were his last hours of freedom.

* * *

He didn't make it through the day. The two police officers who had questioned him after his March trip to the ravine saw the composite, dug through their files, and pulled out Woodcock's dossier. Within an hour, the police were at Woodcock's school.

"When I was in Grade 11, the police mercifully put an end to my career and my education, and, in some ways, I was glad they did. I was having trouble with algebra and geometry, and the further I got into my academic standings, it was becoming more apparent that I was coming to a point of no return that I could not have crossed. I think that I would have come to it in three more days, if I had not been arrested. There was a chapter in the Mathematics book called Quadratic Asserts and Polysyllabic Equations. I read the chapter ahead, but I couldn't

Peter Woodcock is escorted into court, April 1957.

Photo: *Toronto Telegram/Ottawa Sun*

Courtesy: *Toronto Star*

Composite drawing of Peter Woodcock that was printed in the *Toronto Telegram*. It helped police catch the teenage killer.

understand any of it. My brother explained it to me, my father explained it to me, to them it was simple and straightforward, but to me there was a red sign that said Stop and I knew then that I could not go beyond that point.

"It didn't have anything to do with the murders, per se, but what could I tell my folks? Even in Grade 11, I didn't know what I wanted to do with my life. I knew I wanted to go to California. That's all. Things were very tense. I was deeply concerned with being caught. The fantasies, the urges, the compulsions, the obsessions, were all in full force. I was still holding down high marks in History, Latin, English composition.

"It was on my mind every day that I could be caught. I was looking over my shoulder every time that I saw a police cruiser behind me. And my fear was that Mother would find out. Mother was my biggest fear. I didn't know if the police would let her at me.

"After I got caught, I explained it all to her and she was just horrified. She had no idea that she had put me under such pressure. But they did stand by me. If I had been released, I think they would have sent me abroad. Mother was from Maryland, and she knew how they took care of children that had been disgraced. My biggest fear before I was captured was that she would find out first. I knew that whatever she said would be at full decibels, conducted at the highest volume."

The police protected him from "Mother". In fact, they could barely shut him up. He escorted them to the place where he killed Carole Voyce, then went back to the police station to be questioned. He babbled on about the other two killings and all of the sexual assaults. Police calmed him down long enough to sign a statement.

STATEMENT TO POLICE January 21, 1957:
"The first time this happened was in March. You already know the details about that, about the girl. And from then until now I have actually attacked many children, even though I loved children as a rule. I have felt sexually inclined to — I won't go into the number of cases, but will say there must have been

about 11 or 12 of them before I met the girl, that is for this case. And I took her for a ride, to the viaduct, as you fellows know about it now, where I subdued her, and I don't know what I did, but she was dead before I realized what I had done and that was about it. Do you want to know from the time I left her and so on? You want to know how I subdued her, I suppose. Well, first of all, I choked her. This is very gruesome, I know. Then I stuck my fingers in her eyes. I don't know why I did that. Isn't it awful?

And then I when tried to clamber up the bank I was frightened by what I did and as I clambered up the little gully there, I slipped and my feet hit her head. Then I left her, circled back on the other side, as you saw my tracks, took one last look and left. And that's all. But it happened so suddenly, I don't know. I can tell you right now that I don't want a trial before a jury. The reason why my parents were not aware of my sickness is because I never told them. I was too ashamed. Do you blame me? I feel relieved now that I have told you the truth because I was worried. Whatever happens, I don't want to go home tonight. I don't want to face my parents."

"Signed: Peter Maynard."

It wasn't much of a confession. Much more would come out later. It was, however, enough evidence to get the police through an arraignment and a preliminary hearing. In the middle of the night, they sent Woodcock to the Don Jail.

"I was in a safe area, but it was looked after by regular cons. Nobody ever got me, but I would be pushed down the stone steps going to the medication area by the guards. The jail guards were a very brutal bunch," he says of his nine days in one of the country's toughest jails. He was kept close to the death chamber where, if convicted of first degree murder, he would probably hang.

"The police treated me with the greatest courtesy. I have nothing (drawing out the word) but the greatest (drawing this word out, too) praise for the police officers who handled my situation and me during the trial.

"The jail guards teased me about being hanged. That was expected. I knew I was going to hang. As a matter of fact, my lawyer had the greatest difficulty, when the trial opened up, getting me to plead not guilty. Back then, it was a requirement under the law to plead not guilty if you were asking for an insanity verdict. I wanted to go in and say I was guilty of this terrible set of crimes. I wanted to be sentenced to hang.

"You know, the Diefenbaker government commuted nearly all capital sentences, and I believe, now, that it would have commuted mine. If it had, I would be back on the streets. A commuted capital sentence was twenty years.

"I was in the Don Jail for about nine days, then I went to the Toronto Psychiatric Hospital. I was in jail with a guy named Peter, a hell of a good guy, who had been caught for the same kinds of things I had done. He died here.

"The Don Jail was dismal, but then, it was jail. If you offended, you ended up in jail, and jail was not a Sunday school picnic. The guards would push me down, and sometimes an inmate would make a grab for me through the bars. Even the doctor booted me in the ass several times for what I had done. It sounds terrible, but people thirty-seven years ago would understand it.

"The Toronto Psychiatric Hospital was a haven of peace and quiet after that."

Before being packed off to the hospital, an old stone building on Queen Street, Woodcock had to run a press gauntlet. The day after his arrest, the exhausted boy, covered in a canvas tarpaulin, was brought into a courtroom in the city hall. After that first brush with reporters, he went back to the calmness of the hospital. For Woodcock, the exposure had been tantalizing, but he didn't enjoy it.

"I was really afraid of public humiliation. I think if they put me in stocks, like the old days, it would have been worse than hanging."

Meanwhile, Susan Maynard invited reporters into her house to tell the story of her adoption of the strange child. His foster mother, enraged at the newspaper coverage, was still protective. She was sure that he wasn't legally guilty and that he would be acquitted because of his insanity. Meanwhile, the phone rang steadily with anonymous, threatening calls. Within a day or two, the nasty letters would start arriving and would keep coming for years. The Maynard address had become one of the most famous in Toronto. Susan Maynard blamed the doctors, the social workers and the teachers who had dealt with Peter. Frank Maynard, always the suspiciously invisible man, took to bed. His adoptive father never saw his foster son again, and Peter didn't talk about him. He still doesn't.

The funeral for Carole Voyce was held on the Wednesday after her murder. She wore a new pink dress with long sleeves. Her grandfather, Ernest Voyce, picked out the dress and paid for it.

Psychiatrists put together a long report on Woodcock the month after he was arrested. He told the doctors that he was afraid that his small feet were going to cause him trouble, that he had double jointed ankles. He told them he wanted to move to California.

Once, about a month after his arrest, the doctors and nurses at the psychiatric hospital saw the depth of Woodcock's rage. At about 8 p.m. on the night of 25 February, Woodcock went into the washroom on his ward. A man, another patient, was waiting for him there. He grabbed Woodcock and forced him against the wall, all the while muttering something in his ear. A nurse saw the attack, and, as she moved to break it up, heard "a sudden roar from Peter like someone having a violent epileptic seizure". When she pushed her way past Woodcock's assailant, "there was Peter, pale, with wide, sparkling, vicious eyes and tight lips, vibrating in anger like a snake ready to strike".

The indictment was for first-degree murder. By then, police, psychiatrists and prosecutors agreed that the boy was insane.

"You really don't know your own life until you've been on trial for murder. You learn pretty fast what people think of you. I don't recommend it. When I stood trial, the death penalty was there, on the books, and it was being used. A trial becomes like a game between the Crown and the defence. The judge just sits like a big referee up there.

"The trial was held in Courtroom C in Old City Hall, a very ornate room. Every day, there was the usual morbid crowd, press and the public, too. I sat with my back to them, but sometimes, I kind of looked around. The trial really took four days. The Crown took three and a half days. My lawyer read from my file and called four psychiatrists who said I was nuttier than the proverbial dog."

About seventy-five people, mostly elderly downtown Toronto residents with a few days of free time on their hands, sat in the old City Hall courtroom and watched Woodcock as he rose in the prisoner's box. The boy, now eighteen, pleaded "not guilty" in a loud, clear voice. Court was adjourned for a few minutes while Woodcock's lawyer, John Brooke, and Crown prosecutor Arthur Klein met in the chambers of Ontario Supreme Court justice W.F. Spence. Likely, the three men put the last touches on an agreement on the outcome of the trial: not guilty by reason of insanity. Back then there was only one fate for murderers acquitted by reason of insanity on a murder charge. Woodcock would be shipped off to Penetanguishene for the rest of his life. First, though, the formalities of the trial had to be carried out.

Brooke challenged and dismissed twenty jurors. He was trying to keep out people who might convict Woodcock, no matter how crazy he was. Klein, the prosecutor, dismissed two jurors. Woodcock sat stiffly in the prisoner's box, then stared toward a side door of the courtroom as his now-famous bike was wheeled into the room.

Once the jury was sworn in, judge Spence issued a warning:

"May I stress that your sole duty is to bring in a verdict based on the evidence presented here. There was a terrific amount of publicity in this case. Sweep from your mind everything except that which you hear from the witness box. This is a difficult duty for you."

Woodcock stared at the jury, looking tidy in a blue jacket and grey pants, as Klein outlined his case. Woodcock was being tried only for the murder of Carole Voyce. The prosecutor talked about the mothers' shopping trip that Saturday, about how Carole Voyce's mother had come back to the Auld's apartment and had spent a few hours talking to Johnny's mother while the children played outside. Slowly, Klein explained how Woodcock had come up to the children, how he had talked to them for a few minutes and had left with Carole. Without going into much detail, he outlined the trip to the Bloor Viaduct and the murder. Then he mentioned the witnesses who had seen Woodcock with the girl and, later, had watched Woodcock as he walked his bike along the railway tracks near the murder scene.

Klein, of course, was unlikely to have problems winning the case, since Woodcock had been a cooperative prisoner who had spent the winter eagerly telling the story of his crimes to anyone who asked about them. The law requires two things to be proven in an insanity defence: that the person on trial committed the crime, and that he did not understand the nature and consequences of his action. In other words, Klein couldn't just point to Woodcock and say that he was crazy and should be locked up. He would actually have to prosecute the case. If he thought Woodcock wasn't insane, he had to call testimony to prove the boy's state of mind. Back then, when a sentence to Penetanguishene was effectively life imprisonment, prosecutors didn't fight hard against an insanity verdict. These days, an insanity defence is almost always opposed by prosecutors, unless an accused person is hopelessly psychotic, so crazy he has obviously lost all touch with reason.

Many people had come forward to say they had seen Woodcock that afternoon. The secretary, the railroad watchman, the professor who had been stopped by the crazy young man, the schoolboy who was washing his car had all received subpoenas. They weren't really needed.

After four days, the trial was over, and the judge wrote out his verdict:

IN THE SUPREME COURT OF ONTARIO

Thursday, the 11th.
day of April, 1957

BETWEEN
The Queen and Peter Woodcock

The Accused, Peter Woodcock, having on the 8th, 9th, 10th and 11th days of April, 1957, been brought before this court sitting with a jury at the City of Toronto in the County of York in the Province of Ontario, charged with murder and a jury empanelled having found that the accused was not guilty on account of insanity,

This Court doth order that the accused, Peter Woodcock, be kept in strict custody in Toronto Psychiatric Hospital in the said County of York, until the pleasure of His Honour the Lieutenant Governor of the Province of Ontario shall be known.

Wishart G. Spence, J.

The beautiful cream and red bike, with all of its bells and whistles, was rolled out of the courtroom by a bailiff. It was later given to an orphanage.

No one who had been in that courtroom in the spring of 1957 would have guessed that Woodcock would get the chance to kill again. In time, nearly everything that the jury heard about Woodcock would be glossed over by social workers and psychiatrists, and time would dim the public's memory of his crimes. Time, however, never changed the viciousness in Woodcock or took away his thirst to hurt anyone he could overpower. Nor would time or thirty-five years of psychiatric therapy dull the power of the fantasies that ruled his life. In fact, his treatment would teach him how to con weak men like Bruce Hamill, to bend them to his will, and to make them become his hands, his eyes, his ears, when he killed again.

PLAN X

Susan Maynard may have raised Krueger, but Oak Ridge, the maximum security psychiatric institution in Penetanguishene, Ontario, made him the man he is today. His years there paralleled the evolution of psychiatric treatment and the changing policies toward the "criminally insane".

After the Napoleonic Wars, the British government sent hundreds of maimed army veterans into the Canadian wilderness in a mean scheme to cheat them out of their miserable pensions. The wounded soldiers were offered a deal: free land in the colony and a little cash to get started as farmers in return for giving up the pocket change they were entitled to each month. Those who agreed were mostly Londoners who arrived at Montreal or Toronto and drank away their start-up money. Some of the more adventurous disabled pensioners tried to make a living on small farms near the Penetanguishene naval base, where soldiers slipped them food and blankets and gave them part-time work as labourers and watchmen. Years later, some of their descendants got jobs as guards at Oak Ridge when it opened as Ontario's first hospital for the criminally insane in 1933.

After World War I, perhaps because of the it, there were so many violent, insane men locked in Ontario's jails that there weren't enough cells to hold them. During the Depression, the Ontario government decided to build a new institution in Penetanguishene because it was close enough to Toronto to be convenient, but far enough away to be out of view. The land from the long-closed naval base already had an asylum where mentally ill people raised cattle and grew vegetables.

Oak Ridge is a cleverly designed building. Four two-storey wings, running parallel east to west, are connected by a long corridor that runs north-south. The corridor joining the four wings used to be a visitors centre with hard wooden benches for the families of inmates. That's been replaced by a cafeteria-style room with barred windows. The wings each have an upper and lower ward that runs the full length. Each ward has twenty-eight cells. At the end of the wards is a sun room the width of the entire floor where patients sit when they have nothing else to do, which is most of the time that they're awake. There is a barred window in each cell, but it would be pointless to saw through the bars because anyone climbing out a window would end up in the exercise yards. The fences around the yards are topped with rolls of razor-sharp barbed wire. Security cameras watch over the fields around the building. Sensors also pick up any movement. Some aspects of Oak Ridge's security system are secret. Even photographing the locks on the doors is illegal, and morbid tourists who park on the grounds are urged to move on.

There is only one practical way out: through the gate at the end of each ward, down the main connecting corridor and out the front door. There are several steel bar gates along the way, so escape on that route is only possible if an inmate takes a hostage or has help from outside. In 1965, an inmate was helped to escape by his brother, who smuggled a gun past security guards. The two men handcuffed the main door staff and escaped, but were quickly caught.

Years earlier, another inmate broke out of Oak Ridge at least five times, once by making climbing tools from boards and spikes. He used them to climb over the exercise yard fence. Eventually, his trips over the wire became a kind of sport. In the 1960s, the man was finally released. He never re-offended, and now is a successful car dealer (one trade many psychopaths excel at). Krueger thinks maybe they should have let the man out sooner.

The first Oak Ridge inmates arrived from the Guelph Reformatory in 1933 on a special train. They were let off at the railway station near Penetanguishene's harbour and were force-marched, in chains, to the new building. Along the way, the men climbed the steep hills of the town, each carrying a ball and chain attached to his leg. As they marched along the old military road to the hospital grounds, they passed townspeople who gawked and muttered. Oak Ridge was to provide work for nearly all of the local veterans of World War I, but it also brought notoriety to the community.

The 1930s were a time of radical and quite cruel experimentation in psychiatry. Inmates were subjected to insulin therapy, a dangerous procedure that often nearly killed them. A victim of this treatment was injected with insulin, which brought on a coma, and revived with an injection of glucose, a type of sugar. Another treatment, a drug called metrazol, resulted in violent convulsions. Lobotomies, the killing of a portion of the brain, were a routine operation until the early 1960s. Patients were loaded onto a flatbed truck normally used to haul garbage and taken down the hill to the regional asylum, where surgical tools were thrust into their brain behind the eye, severing the blood flow to the frontal lobe in a matter of seconds. Shock treatments were done so often that patients sometimes lined up in Oak Ridge's corridors, waiting to lie down on an operating table and have massive jolts of electricity sent through their brains. Many people who survived these cruel and usually worthless treatments became vehement opponents of the mental health system and came back, politically and physically, to haunt Oak Ridge. The less fortunate ones wandered the halls of psychiatric hospitals for years, trying to recover their memory.

When they weren't having their brains scrambled by their doctors, the inmates worked on the hospital farm. They grew vegetables that were eaten in Oak Ridge through the winter. Trusted patients walked into town to see movies and went on fishing trips with attendant friends. There were even pets in Oak Ridge, cats from the farm that slipped through the barred front doors and wandered the wards. As long as no one made trouble, the system was allowed to become less restrictive. The old system at Oak Ridge worked if no one challenged the status quo. Peter Woodcock embraced life in this cocoon with enthusiasm. After all, walls and bars keep the world out just as well as they keep prisoners in.

* * *

Woodcock arrived at Penetang at 11:00 a.m. on 20 April, 1957: Good Friday. A form filled out by the hospital's staff showed he had normal temperature, pulse and respiration. He was five feet, five and a half inches tall (he's shrunk somewhat since them), weighed one hundred and five pounds, had hazel eyes and black hair. He was clean, with no noticeable vermin. He carried with him an electric razor and a nail file, which were turned over to the hospital bursar for safekeeping. In Woodcock's suitcase was a bathrobe, three Bibles, a suit, a pair of eyeglasses, a handkerchief, and some street clothes.

Less than a month after Woodcock arrived at Oak Ridge, he was taken back to Toronto. Finally, justice was about to be done for Ron Mowatt, the boy who had been jailed in the dreadful

Guelph Reformatory for the murder of Wayne Mallette. A few days before the hearing, three men had come to see Woodcock: his lawyer, John Brooke; a Mr. Hartt, who was the lawyer for Mowatt; and a Metro police officer, all of whom wanted to be sure that Woodcock would testify to his guilt. There was some foot-dragging by Oak Ridge officials. Some of them believed that Woodcock might be confessing to a crime that he had read about in the newspapers.

For a week, Woodcock was in Toronto, staying at the old Queen Street asylum. At the end of a short hearing in one of Toronto's City Hall courtrooms, Mowatt was finally set free. He had spent half a year locked up for a murder he didn't commit, and for more than half of that time, the authorities knew that he was innocent. If Woodcock had stopped his killings after the death of Wayne Mallette, or even while the police were still puzzling over the Gary Morris case, Mowatt would never have been cleared.

Mowatt's mother told newspapers that her son had been through hell: drug treatments by doctors who believed he was lying about his innocence; a trial that ended in a miscarriage of justice; months locked up as a child murderer, at the bottom of the Guelph reform school pecking order. There would, however, be no compensation or apology. At the end of the hearing, Mowatt was given back to his sobbing parents. In 1957, that was as much as he or his family could hope for.

"My boy is innocent and my prayers have been answered that a new development would come in the case," his mother said to the same reporters who had worked with the police to put Mowatt away.

Going back over Woodcock's file, I saw lingering doubts among some of his therapists that Woodcock committed the Mallette murder. At times, Woodcock himself seemed unclear in his interviews with psychiatrists. He would sometimes act as though he didn't trust his memory, and say that, since he worked Saturday nights at Casa Loma, he might not have been able to commit the crime. If that was so, then, perhaps, another killer might have gone free. It wasn't likely, but the possibility remained.

One day in the summer of 1996, when Krueger phoned me to chatter about something trivial, I decided to ask him if he killed Wayne. He was in a rather jovial mood, happier than he had been in several weeks. The hospital had issued an edict earlier in the summer that he quit telling jokes to other patients. That rule had been lifted.

So, did he kill Wayne Mallette?

"Oh, yes," he said.

Why did he bother helping Mowatt get out of jail?

"I was really angry that he was taking credit for something I did. It had bothered me since he was arrested, but I couldn't exactly come forward, could I?"

* * *

The summer and early fall of 1957 were a time of adjustment for Woodcock, and things didn't always go well. In the spring, he was lonely and worried. No one who had committed murder, he was told, was ever released from Oak Ridge. Within weeks, though, he began feeling safe, despite his tiny size. Many of the other inmates, out of pity or lust, were kind. During the summer, he enjoyed the attention paid to him by four homosexual inmates who courted him and quarrelled with each other. By October, however, he was depressed. He managed to get about a half metre of copper wire from an electrical cord, tie it into knots, and insert it deep into his penis. Attendants rushed to the screaming boy's room to find him lying on his cot, bleeding. They tried to pull the wire out, but it wouldn't budge. The next morning, when the Oak Ridge doctor arrived, he was given the task of removing the copper strip. Woodcock was given a "whiff of anaesthesia", according to his medical report, and the doctor gave the wire a stiff pull. Woodcock spent the rest of the day in a cold bath.

Oak Ridge staff tried to cover up the self-mutilation. When Susan Maynard came to visit a few days later, she saw that Peter was unwell, but he told her that he had the flu. The institution's staff supported the lie, saying that a cold virus was sweeping through Oak Ridge's wards.

Still, Susan Maynard worried. Just after Woodcock's first Christmas in Oak Ridge, she sent a plaintive letter to his psychiatrist. For the next ten years, there was a steady stream of correspondence, but by the late 1960s, it tapered off. Krueger doesn't know what happened to Susan Maynard and the rest of his foster family.

By the late fall of 1957, Woodcock's groin had healed. He broke out of his funk and became one of the busiest homosexuals on his ward, constantly in trouble for being in other men's rooms. Through the next couple of years, he developed the routine that he loves so much: time with his friends, a few hours listening to radio, and working in the Oak Ridge library or kitchen. Woodcock always shies away from physical labour, and even in the library, where he could look through books all day, he was known as a slacker. He was more enthusiastic for the Oak Ridge newspaper, the *Quill*, and he liked to run the projector on movie nights. What he really enjoyed was the routine, the sense that everything, like the streetcars, was running on schedule.

"In the late '50s, we got up at 7:15 in the morning. The first sign that the day was beginning was when the day shift chief and the night shift chief walked in pairs down the wards, to do the count. The day shift could not open up the cells until that count was completed," he says.

"They would open up our doors between 7:15 and 7:30. By eight o'clock, breakfast was done, and you were expected to help in the cleanup. If you did, you got some tobacco, and that was a good motivator. Then you went back to your cell and sat on your bed and listened to the ward radio. It was under lock and key. So was the TV, which was only allowed to be on from seven until nine, Wednesday to Sunday. And it only got one channel.

"Lunch time was 11:30, right on the dot. When that was over, you went back and lay down and, if you had a magazine, you read it. Some people were allowed to play cards. At one o'clock, yard would be called, and if you didn't go, you were locked in your cell. Yard went from 1:30 and went to 4:15, seven days a week, in the spring and summer. If the other guys were playing baseball, you had a wonderful time dodging the fly balls. A newspaper would arrive in the evening, one for each ward, and it was thrown out the next morning. It was a very dull place, and nothing changed.

"Dinner was early, and by five o'clock, you would be locked up in your cell until seven, when you could go down and watch the television. If you didn't, you would be locked in your room. By nine, everyone was locked up for the night. This was the same, every day of the week, month in, month out, year in, year out.

"Yard was shut down at the end of Labour Day and opened again on Victoria Day. The rest of the year, you did the same thing in the afternoon that you did in the morning: read a magazine, listen to the radio, go down and play cards. It was a long day."

Ten years into his stay, after dozens of sexual relations, obsessions, run-ins with staff, and little acts of defiance and craziness, he was described in a report as a patient always looking for other inmates to have sex with, a braggart who expected other patients to be impressed by his crimes, but who, at the same time, told staff that he felt remorse. His work in the typing and print shop was sloppy. He had full privileges, including the right to send and receive letters and have visitors, but few of either came for Woodcock. In the summer of 1967, he became obsessed with yet another patient, Steven Jones, who had spent time hanging around with the hippy crowd in Toronto's Yorkville counter-culture colony. The object of Woodcock's desire didn't share Peter's enthusiasm.

Woodcock followed the young man around "like a puppy", according to a social worker's report. Other inmates wanted the new patient, too. Woodcock reacted by sending them anonymous threatening letters. This was not a bright move by a small, nearsighted inmate without many friends. At least one fight broke out, which ended when Woodcock grabbed something sharp and cut a patient who was trying to restrain him.

The next year, his affections had settled on someone else. David Lesperance seems to have returned Woodcock's feelings, the two of them going so far as to agree to "Plan X", a suicide pact. When the guards found out about Plan X, Woodcock ended up shackled and locked up in a strip safe-room, a cell with nothing in it but a cement slab to sleep on and an untearable denim blanket for warmth. Later, he was transferred to intensive therapy, and, by late summer, was back in his old cell. Lesperance returned to Woodcock's ward a few months later. Desperate now, Woodcock took what little money he had and bought mod clothes. He let his hair grow long and tried to act like a hippy. It was no use: by Christmas, Lesperance had taken up with another inmate. Woodcock schemed to kill them both. Soon, however, he dropped that plan. There was too much going on around him. At the end of the 1960s, the counterculture had arrived at Penetanguishene. A crack had opened in the doors of Oak Ridge. Killers were starting to be released, and the place was becoming much more interesting for the inmates who were still inside.

* * *

PROGRESS REPORT
April 2, 1967 (Dr. Barker-J.G)
Progress notes compiled by patients: LOWE, TUCKER & MASON
Period Covered: October 1966 - March 1967

28-year-old Peter came to Oak Ridge 120 months ago, and has been living on G Ward for fourteen months. Pale, short, thin and intense, Peter has received no treatment for physical illness in the six months covered by this report.

MEDICATION: He has received no tranquilizers, but drugs have been administered to disrupt his defences. In December 1966 he was given 30 mg. Methedrine I.M. and in January 2 Dexamyl Spansules, #2 caps. were given daily for a period of 15 days.

SYMPTOMS: His participation in treatment programs has been moderately good. Generally, he responds well when requested, but does not volunteer himself freely. He carries himself with a tense sort of confidence and tends to act in an artificially authoritative manner when on "official" business. While warm and friendly at times, he can become withdrawn and very suspicious when he feels his security to be threatened, and characteristically in the past chose to suppress much of the fear and resentment that he felt of staff and other "prestigious" patients.

Generally, he presents the picture of a moderately integrated schizophrenic person, vacillating rapidly between the barbed insecurity of his own fantasy and the apparently uncaring world.

The highlights of his recent development was the Dexamyl treatments of January which appeared to allow him a much freer expression of hostility. He approached significant others with an aggressiveness and "openness" that appeared sometimes to be forced, but overall with more confidence than formerly. In the last month, he talked with unaccustomed violence about "punching people in the mouth", and in small groups his discussions of his sexual imaginations and fantasies has broadened to the point where he describes in detail his sexual feelings about specific ward members.

Periodically, he produces disproportionate amounts of emotional at inappropriate times, and while he can talk freely about such things, his insight into them often appears to be limited or invented. His relationships with many ward members appear to be dominated by a strong, conscious sexual component, but on closer examination we wonder if the powerful sexual feelings he describes are quite as important to him as his ideas that perhaps he means nothing to anybody.

He reports considerable guilt about his crime, but his behaviour suggests little experiencing of it. Predominant among his thoughts appear to be fantasies of power and possession, together with some ideas about his illness that appear to be slightly delusional. He speaks of feeling better equipped to defend himself when wearing heavy boots, for example, and puts them on ritually; he speaks of not wanting to lose his illness because it is all he has left; he speaks of "ruler of the universe" fantasies; occasionally he will appear subtly to brag about his crime; there are times when he is convinced people do not care, in spite of their apparently sincere statements to the contrary. At other times, he will be pliant to the point of agreeing with a point of view rather than risk the loss of a friend.

He is employed in the typing and printing room, where his work is inconsistent and careless. Inaccurate and unable to follow instructions closely, he often appears more interested in creating status for himself than in working. His personal habits are rather careless and his room is an untidy reservoir of records and magazines which he appears to hoard almost defensively.

He receives no mail or visits.

TREATMENT: 1 Methedrine treatment; 15 Dexamyl treatments. 27 small groups, 20 days observation.

CHANGES: Increased aggressiveness, more open discussion of sexual and homicidal fantasies, and increased readiness to relax controls on himself, suggest a loosening of internal defence that promises well for Peter's development. He appears to be more ready to assert his own needs in a direct, openly emotional way, than by means of fantasy or daydreaming. His insight into himself and others appears to have increased and while much of this seems to be of a rather spurious intellectual sort, its appearance is favourable.

PROGNOSIS: Continued reality-testing of long repressed emotions will lead to Peter's realizing much of his potential. Intensive milieu therapy of at least two years' duration we would expect to be of some benefit.

* * *

Plato believed in archetypal evil, that evil was a measurable component of a person, just like water. A man or woman might evolve in other ways as they grew older, but the evil stayed inside, like something indigestible. Today, philosophers, psychiatrists and criminologists argue whether a person can have real evil within him, be evil right to the core of his being. Is evil something that is built into a person's make-up, controllable perhaps, but always there? Or are people like Krueger suffering from a disease that can be treated, a handicap that can be overcome by purging the person of the psychological or organic flaw that drove them to commit hideous crimes?

The psychiatrists who ran Oak Ridge in the 1960s believed psychopaths like Woodcock might be curable. Peal back the layers of the personality of Woodcock and the other psychopaths in Oak Ridge, cure their corrupt thinking patterns and beliefs, and they could be re-assembled as honest people. Psychiatry, especially its drugs, was evolving so fast that doctors were now able to treat mental disorders that, less than a decade earlier, would have sent a person to an institution for life. And more new treatments were on the horizon. The researchers just didn't realize how deep the sickness of someone like Woodcock goes. Like an interstellar black hole or a bottomless pit, no one would ever be able to reach a solid core of Woodcock's psyche and be able to say, "we know what's here".

The government of Ontario liked the idea of treating and releasing long-term inmates. Oak Ridge was expensive to run, overcrowded, and the number of men who were being sent there was increasing as the province's population grew. It's interesting to note that the number of people in Ontario has risen from less than four million to nearly ten million since Oak Ridge opened, yet it's still the only institution of its kind in Ontario, with half the beds that it had in the 1960s.

In the post-war years, until the pendulum swung to the right in the 1980s, social attitudes towards locking people up for the rest of their lives had softened. People realized that most prisoners who are incarcerated for more than a decade are unable to cope with freedom. One retired attendant who worked at Oak Ridge in the early 1960s says he remembers taking an old patient on a drive a week or so before the man was released. The inmate, who had been locked in Oak Ridge since the Depression, looked across the farm fields and asked, "where did all the horses go?"

Oak Ridge didn't release anyone accused of murder until 1962. These inmates were killers who were so feeble that they couldn't harm anyone.

About the time that Oak Ridge began releasing murderers, Dr. Elliot Barker arrived at the institution. The new psychiatrist, only thirty-one-years-old, had just graduated from the University of Toronto. Dr. Barker was, and still is, a bright, friendly man with few pretensions and a skill for listening. He had specialized in the leading edge therapeutic community research that psychiatrists hoped could offer cures to the chronic mentally ill. Oak Ridge was to be turned into one of the world's boldest experiments in patient-run therapy.

Psychopaths were recruited from the jails to run the patients' side of the program. Dr. Barker and other Oak Ridge staff went to court and testified on their behalf when they pleaded not guilty by reason of insanity. Oak Ridge also put the word out to prisons to send their most heartless, uncaring inmates to Penetanguishene.

Patients spent as much as eighty hours a week in intensive therapy. These sessions weren't stereotypical visits with a psychiatrist or a group of well-meaning, neurotic people talking about their fears. They were all-day verbal brawls between gangs of shouting inmates who focused on one patient and demanded he show emotions and feelings. While conventional psychiatry tried to dampen down the craziness of patients and ease their troubled minds, the Oak Ridge therapeutic community tried to bring it out to be analyzed and dealt with. Any sign of dishonesty or evasion was punished, often brutally. There was no mercy for the weak.

"Dyads", locking two men in a room together for an hour a day, every day, was supposed to create feelings of care and concern in people who could kill on a whim. Patients who began to crumble and realize the horror of their illnesses and crimes were carefully watched by other patients to make sure they didn't commit suicide. If the inmate committees believed a man was a high risk, he was shackled to another patient who became responsible for looking after the despondent inmate. The patients were even involved in the design of the handcuffs, which were made from scraps from a nearby seatbelt factory. In the sunrooms at the end of the ward, suicide risks were shackled to beds at night while their patient protectors stood over them.

"In the therapeutic communities under Dr. Barker, his idea was to keep everybody on edge, on the thin edge of the razor," Krueger says. "Chaos was always the anticipated result, so you had to guard against that. And because people encountered their emotions in the raw, with full force, they could start swinging. The goal was to introduce you to your emotions, and try to teach you ways of controlling them that would help you live a more effective life, more meaningful for yourself. Most people who are mentally ill have a problem with their feelings and their emotions. So we were taught here to think whatever you like, but don't act on it, don't hit anybody. Act normal. The difference between the program here and the snake-pit horror at other hospitals was that they wanted to see your feelings, but if you became violent, you were punished. Every time you blundered at St. Thomas (Psychiatric Hospital, near London, Ontario), where they sent me for a few months, you were punished."

Dr. Barker and his colleagues justified the harsh regime:

"The ostensible barbarism of procedures which involve direct physical restraint can often obscure their advantages in therapy, clouding the perhaps greater but less obtrusive violence of chemical, electrical and architectural restraints.

"That they effectively reduce the risks of homicide and suicide is, of course, the major justification for handcuffs, but other advantages disive [sic] from their employment. The patient is continuously in the presence of his friends and enemies, no matter what he does, an arrangement which builds a powerful and unavoidable bond between the individual and his group. Regardless of the degree of upset, he can remain in a group of his peers to talk (or shout) about his feelings if he wishes. He remains mobile, may participate in all activities, and may feel better at having been cared for by his peers rather than by staff, gaining perhaps some ego-enhancement from the attention."

Alcohol, scopolamine, sodium amaytal, speed, and LSD were used to try to expose the inner turmoil of patients and to force the patients who weren't using the drugs to look after the inmates who were. Dr. Barker gave patients whisky to probe their feelings, or even to find out if they had any at all. For months, three to five patients were undergoing heavy drug therapy at any one time. Friends and enemies of a drugged patient would visit him to try to bring out emotions. When a patient began to get tired, he would be injected with amphetamines. At night, he was kept in the "Intensive Care Unit", a makeshift mini-ward in the sunroom at the end of an Oak Ridge cell block. Tranquilizers were rarely used, since tranquillity, in the short term, was not a goal of the therapeutic community.

Ideally, Barker wrote, "the inmate should be allowed no experience that does not in some way contribute to his re-education, and every minute of his stay should be designed intentionally to bring about a change in his ability to cope when he is released." Any inmate who threw the community off-balance by trying to bring undue attention on himself was punished. The penalties inflicted by patient committees ranged from writing a 1,000 word essay to being transferred to the MAP program, a place no one, no matter how crazy, wanted to go.

In the MAP program, the punitive aspects of the therapeutic community came out. It was the flip side to the democratic system that operated in the wards below. Patients had no personal belongings. They lived in the simplest cells and slept on a concrete slab until they earned the privilege of a thin mattress and a blanket made of denim. MAP inmates wore "baby doll" gowns made of tough cloth. The gown was designed to be difficult to use as a rope for a suicide. Sometimes inmates were left in their cells for months. When they were allowed out, patients were subjected to brutal sessions organized by psychopaths and staff. Usually, they were shackled in a fetal position and forced to crouch upright for days. If they fell over, the inmates on the punishment crew would force them upright again. No magazine or newspaper reporters ever went to MAP, but the patients who did end up there learned quickly that they were locked in a very nasty institution.

Peter Woodcock was one of the inmates who screened new patients when they arrived:

"If you were coming in off the street, you would be met at the gate by a big attendant who had been through both world wars and had the beer gut to prove it. He would shake your hand and say 'welcome to Oak Ridge'. Then you would be would plunked down in front of the assessment committee, whose members were chosen from the more articulate patients. The committee would be sitting around a table, maybe a couple of murders, two or three rapists and an arsonist. They would ask you your name, why you were here. Then would want to know if you think you could fit in. The questions were polite, but if they didn't like the answers, if you got defensive, things could turn nasty very quickly."

In fact, the psychopathic patients who ran the program used the training unit to prove their power, to show new inmates that the therapeutic community was no joke, and that the roof would fall in on anyone who acted like it was. They badgered the prison codes of ethics out of the new patients and taught them some of the psychobabble they would need later on. The new arrivals also learned to keep their mouth shut until they were out of H-Ward, the row of cells where they stayed when they arrived. This block had none of the amenities of the rest of the hospital, and was not meant to be a place to become attached to. Once someone agreed to go into the therapeutic community, usually for a minimum of six months, there was no way out.

In the therapeutic community, Peter Woodcock, murderous geek and bottom-feeding toady, evolved into David Michael

Krueger, socially skilled, manipulative leader. He learned the fine arts of coercion, refined his ability to lie, strengthened his fantasy life, and developed new ways to exploit his fellow inmates. These new skills were to prove lethal.

* * *

All activities in Oak Ridge were governed by rules drafted in 1960s psychobabble. Woodcock's files show that, on May 5, 1972, "Peter was sanctioned for not feeding back about keeping watch while Melvin Paice and John Ross engaged in mutual masturbation. Peter stated that as much as he enjoys homosexuality he did not act out, although he has once in the past year."

What was the sin here? Keeping watch? Not snitching? Not snitching on himself for keeping watch? Being homosexual? "Acting out" once in the past year? Anyone could be blamed for being confused when trying to fathom this kind of talk?

Dr. Barker's ideas of crowding men together to bring out their emotions of anger, fear and hate generated "The Hundred-Day Hate-In", an experiment that was supposed to hurry the effects of intense therapy. In the subsequent academic paper he wrote describing the experiment, Dr. Barker feared that if he jacked up the stress levels on the wards, patients would use the "veritable armoury" of steel bedsprings, glass coffee jars, sheets, chairs, forks and spoons they had stashed in their cells on each other or themselves. As well, psychopaths would busy themselves running high-stress therapy sessions for other people and not be affected by it themselves. Dr. Barker was told by psychopaths that they could resist change as long as there was some time during the week that they were alone to read or watch television. In the regular therapeutic community, they still had enough privacy to preserve their own personalities.

So Dr. Barker locked up sixteen volunteers in a sunroom stripped of all of its furniture and books. They were warned before they went in that the program would be tough, and they signed a contract saying they would stick it out. No one was allowed to bring tobacco in, and most of the patients in Oak

Ridge were, and are, heavy smokers. That meant the stress level would start off high. While the patients were in the Hate-In, they couldn't leave. No one was allowed to talk to the attendants outside the door, to receive letters or see visitors. Food was eaten from paper plates with paper spoons, and was shoved into the room through a slot in the door. The room was kept brightly lit at night, and patients were guarded by inmates who were kept awake on speed. By the fourth day, patients were begging to be let out. Some tried demands, threats, cajoling, but the Hate-In was for real. No one was going anywhere.

The first group in the Hate-In actually survived being locked up together for 100 days. Guards remember seeing patients who were normally cold and strong becoming raving men whose fear and anger revealed itself in terrifying eruptions of rage. Others sat staring out the window at the groundhogs wandering the fields, or strangled flies with a piece of thread. Paranoid patients began to believe that the other men in the Hate-In were hiding something from them. Even after the inmates were given amphetamines, they gradually spoke less often to each other. Many just slept or sat around. Most just didn't seem to care about anything.

"I'll shine people's shoes, but I can't love them," a patient wrote after he was let out of the Hate-In.

* * *

Soon, Dr. Barker came up with a new, improved encounter group theory, based partly on what he learned from the One Hundred Day Hate-In. The Compressed Encounter Capsule was a sort of artificial womb where patients were kept so close together that conflict, even attempted murder, was expected to be inevitable. Patients went into the eight-by-ten-foot capsule for up to three weeks. They were searched for weapons, although one patient did get in with a razor blade hidden under his false-teeth plate. Sometimes Barker injected his subjects with LSD, other times they went in straight. Hot and cold liquid food came into the capsule through straws thrust through holes in the door, adding to its womb-like ambience. The lights never went off. Patients were supposed to lose track of time, but the clanging of doors on the wards could be heard inside the tiny room.

The tiny space was supposed to be an incentive for cooperation. Patients fought to strip away the defences of their fellow capsule mates. Sometimes they were handcuffed together to try to speed up the process, or as a punishment for violence and sexual advances. The decision to cuff a patient was made by a majority vote of the other capsule inmates. Capsule sessions were filmed by other patients who watched the encounters through two-way mirrors.

Krueger really liked LSD. So did Dr. Barker and many other philosophers and psychiatrists engaged in treatment experiments during the 1960s. In fairness to Dr. Barker, Woodcock and the treatment program, LSD was believed by many people in 1967 to be an easy route to the subconscious. Dr. Barker's work wasn't the brainwashing experiments of the CIA in the 1950s, where the memories and personalities of mental patients were completely erased. The Penetanguishene team believed they could tap into a well of feelings that psychopaths managed to keep locked inside. They shouldn't be blamed for trying to treat these men. For all anyone knew at the time, it could have worked.

No enthusiast of street drugs could imagine the ride that the psychopaths in Penetanguishene went on. Pure LSD was combined with speed for two-day trips, no sleep, just non-stop hallucinations. Woodcock went into the capsule on Nov. 9, 1970. He was given Gravol, followed fifteen minutes later by the LSD.

"On the first trip. I was sitting there with my guide, who was a schizophrenic, the same as myself, and I had become aware that there was this wizard, this black hooded figure, over me. You know, in the Sorcerer's Apprentice, like Mickey (Mouse) in Fantasia. I thought, what was that? There was a feeling of deep foreboding, but I also knew that was part of me. And then, all of a sudden, I was into it, there was a rushing feeling, and there were all these dancing dots. It took me a long time to realize that it was a television screen with no picture. My awareness of all these dots, this rushing sound, like when you turn a TV to an empty channel. My memory breaks up into sequentials.

"I remember they brought in some people to see how I would react to them. There was one fellow who was quite young, of whom I was inordinantly fond of. When he held my hand, I thought I could feel something unravelling. I could feel his hand, and I know he could feel mine. I figured there was this chasm between us that could not be bridged, and this feeling was the bond being taken away. I could see the changes I had made, and that showed me I was okay, despite all the terrible feelings I had about myself.

"But I got into a trap. I was walking along a beautiful country road on a warm day in July, looking out across fields that went to the horizon. I got to a fork in the road, and there was an old gaffer sitting on a bridge. I would ask him which way to go. He wouldn't say anything, he would just point. I would start walking and come across him again. He would just point, and I would keep going. The same thing kept happening over and over.

"Somehow, Dr. Barker figured out what was happening, and he shot me up with methydrene. That was when things really took off. It was a very comforting experience, for a while, but then I became depressed. I kept thinking about the crimes against the children, and hearing 'no sense, no sense, no sense'. Then I finally realized that it was just people saying 'nonsense'.

"Then the trip takes off in a totally different direction. I can see all of the veins in my legs and arms. I had an awful feeling. It was very startling, and I jerked back. I felt very warm, and I saw smoke in front of my eyes. After a while, I became aware that I was no longer having any physical feelings. I looked at my body, and I had become a pile of bones. I became two or three little circles, floating in this very bright light. Then I reached the light.

"I should never say this, but the experience left me with no feelings or emotions. When I reached the lights, I felt okay. I was aware I was sitting on something very hard, and I felt like I was in a great crystal room, sitting at something like a computer console, where everything was made out of crystal. Everything was beautiful. After several more experiences that I can't recall, I remember hearing some music, a fast little item from the jazz days. I was in a shop where all of these teddy bears were dancing. I hate teddy bears. It was really aggravating because they wouldn't stop.

"I started thinking about things: my guide, he was all fractured. I had a feeling of coming down a spiral, and I remember lying there, aware of where I was externally, but internally, my arms and my legs had their own intelligence. I remember that, if I wanted to move, I had to ask one of these intelligences. And that was it, I began getting control over my limbs, and I was pretty much out of it."

"I tried to get up. I felt nauseated, with a horrible taste of banana in my mouth. I've hated bananas ever since."

In the end, LSD didn't do much for Krueger except make him depressed. The experiments continued at Penetanguishene long after researchers elsewhere had realized that the "insights" that people got on the drug were just symptoms of changes in brain chemistry. A new researcher, Dr. Gary Maier, not only embraced the experiments at Penetanguishene, he took them much farther. Dr. Maier was a believer in eastern mysticism who brought the *Tibetan Book of the Dead* into Oak Ridge. The guards didn't like Dr. Maier. His bosses were ready to give him a chance, believing that, among the therapies he was trying, there might be some that worked on people who were, in the eyes of society, garbage to be thrown away.

Dr. Barry Boyd, who was still chief psychiatrist, would later write:

"As long as Elliott (Barker) was here he had a new idea almost every week. I remember the day he came to me with the Capsule. He and I worked awfully well as a team. I knew what he was doing and I was ready to support him. His successor, Dr. Gary Maier, was a very brilliant young fellow who is now having a great career down in Wisconsin. His ideas were even farther out. He was into some of the Eastern philosophies and the *Tibetan Book of the Dead*.

"That stuff could be dynamite if certain people got hold of it — they could say that we were trying to brainwash people with religious ideas, but we just thought it was something the patients could share with enthusiasm together, as they shared their feelings and talked. Once he had the whole ward standing around, staring at their navels going 'Oooommm'. I had to make darned sure if the Minister (of Health) was visiting I didn't take him in to witness that scene!"

Finally, in 1976, an illegal strike by guards at Oak Ridge ended with Dr. Maier and most of his treatment team being expelled from the institution. Dr. Barker stayed on as an Oak Ridge therapist, working part-time with a few patients and assessing men sent to Oak Ridge before their trials. Dr. Barker decided that psychopathy could only be cured by attacking its source, which, he believes, is lack of nurturing of infants. His efforts are now directed, through the Society for the Prevention of Cruelty to Children, toward educating people about the need for families and societies that value and cherish children. In his will, Krueger has left all his assets to Barker's organization.

"By the time I left Oak Ridge in 1973, I was preoccupied with what was worth doing with the rest of my life," Dr. Barker told me in an interview. "I had a couple of meal tickets as a doctor and a psychiatrist. I kept coming back to that idea that society didn't realize that the early years are incredibly important. In the 1970s, there was much less awareness of that than there is now. I was posing the question 'If you can take a child for three years, what three-year block of time would have the most influence on them?' The answers were coming back '12 to 15', 'seven to 10'. It was crazy. If you think about the first three years of life, and the pregnancy leading up to them, it's obvious that the first three years of life are very critical."

Daycare became one of Dr. Barker's targets. His organization publishes articles and booklets on issues such as long-term breast feeding, coping mechanism for parents, and the need for infants to have a stable relationship with at least one parent through the first three years of life.

"For about ten per cent of the population, who were so crazy that they completely screw their kids up, day care is a good thing for kids. But for the rest of the population, it's crazy to separate kids from the six people who can look after children: parents and grandparents. They're the only people who will put in the irrational amount of work that is required to raise a child.

"Nobody else will or can. It doesn't take a village to raise a child, it takes parents."

* * *

The new management that took over Oak Ridge after the experimental team was expelled decided the psychopaths belonged on the street or in jail, not in a hospital, so they started shipping them to medium security psychiatric hospitals, which, in turn, prepped them for release. Time has proven that the treatment experiments were failures. Studies by the Oak Ridge research department show they made Krueger and his colleagues better criminals. They learned new skills to con the gullible, and how to co-operate more efficiently when they planned crimes. In most criminal trials, psychiatrists testified that psychopaths were sane, that they belonged in prison. For people like Krueger, prison was a death sentence, and the street was nearly as bad. Krueger's keepers had raised a person, now entering middle age, who could never function as a free man, who had no hopes of holding a job, had no skills to live in his own home, and whose diamond-hard core of murderous fantasies had survived all of the attempts to purge them.

* * *

Krueger wasn't alone. Oak Ridge had dozens of inmates who could never be trusted again. A few of them made headlines in the next few years, but Oak Ridge simply weathered the storms of public anger and kept emptying its wards.

Cecil Gillis was twenty-five-years old when the police arrested him for the 1974 murder of a young Etobicoke woman, Laverne Merle Johnson, at a park near Parry Sound. By then, he was already one of Canada's worst serial killers. Gillis had killed eight women in British Columbia, then had hitch-hiked across the country. He had joined the volunteer team that had searched for Johnson. Gillis was caught when he gave fellow searchers hints to the location of Johnson's body, which lay, raped and mutilated, below a bridge. Within twelve years of his capture, Gillis was through Ontario's forensic mental health system and back on the streets, though not for long.

Robert Abel arrived at Oak Ridge about the same time as Gillis, after bludgeoning his wife and two young children to death in the southern Ontario community of Chatham. He and Gillis were the same age, though Abel was much larger and stronger than Gillis. Abel, worn out by booze and dugs, looked older. On the day before his mother's birthday, Abel had phoned her to say he was going to give her a present she would never forget. Then he sat down and wrote a letter to her, saying his children "shouldn't have to live in a world where no one cares about each other." The next day, police found him unconscious among the bodies of his wife and children.

After about four years in Oak Ridge, Gillis and Abel were transferred to the 400-bed St. Thomas Psychiatric Hospital, south of London. The two men, who had barely known each other in Oak Ridge, became friends while they spent seven years in the St. Thomas hospital's medium security wing. They knew how to behave, so they were given day passes to leave the hospital to work. Gillis found a labouring job in a factory near the hospital. After a few months, he had enough money to buy a car.

On an early spring afternoon, Gillis told his boss at the Sparta Mercantile factory that he wanted to "leave early and get laid." That night, Thursday, March 31, 1988, he and Abel began wandering the roads around St. Thomas. "I went to the liquor store and got a jug of Kelly's and went to the park, went to see my old friend, a tree, and have a drink with him," Abel later said. They cruised the streets of London. Just after it got dark, Gillis and Abel stopped in a driveway next to a fourteen-year-old girl who was waiting for a bus. The girl realized something was wrong when Gillis got out of the car and walked toward her. She tried to run away, but Gillis caught her and jammed her into the front seat of the car between himself and Abel, who was blind drunk. Gillis drove south out of the city, beating the girl as he tried to keep the car on the road. They travelled thirty kilometres to the factory where Gillis worked. Once there, Gillis viciously raped the girl. Abel sat in the car and kept drinking.

After the attack, Gillis told the girl to put her clothes back on. When she wasn't looking, he moved behind her and choked her into unconsciousness. The men drove along country roads with the sleeping teenager in the back seat. Gillis pulled off the road at an isolated bridge over Catfish Creek, near the psychiatric hospital. As Gillis dragged the girl from the car, Abel, who couldn't stand up, sat in the drivers' seat and begged Gillis not to kill her. In the darkness, Abel saw Gillis swing the unconscious girl several times and roll her over the handrail at the centre of the bridge. She fell seven metres into the shallow creek, striking her face on the rocks. Gillis grabbed Abel's arm and started dragging him toward the creek.

"I'll do the same thing to you if you tell anybody," he said to Abel, who was so drunk he could barely struggle. Gillis pushed Abel onto the passenger seat, got in, and drove off.

Whether it was the force of the fall or the cold water that awoke her, something caused Gillis' victim to regain consciousness. She struggled from the river and climbed up the bank with blood pouring from her face. The girl managed to find a farmhouse nearby and went inside. No one was home, so the girl, who was losing consciousness again, wandered from room to room, turning on the lights. An hour later, the people who owned the house came home, found her and called the police. The teenager spent three weeks in hospital and needed plastic surgery for the injuries to her face.

Gillis and Abel, who were sure the girl was dead, signed in late at the St. Thomas hospital. They went to their rooms and fell asleep. The next day, with the story of the attack in every Ontario newspaper and on the radio, Gillis turned himself in to the police. He was charged with attempted murder, abduction and sexual assault causing bodily harm.

Police arrested Abel a few hours later and took him back to Oak Ridge. In a hearing that lasted only a few minutes, Gillis pleaded guilty to attempted murder and aggravated sexual assault. In June 1989, Gillis was declared a dangerous offender. Under Canadian law, criminals who are declared dangerous are sent to federal penitentiaries, where they are allowed hearings every two years to determine if they are safe to be released. Gillis is now being held in a maximum security prison near Kingston, Ontario.

Another Oak Ridge alumnus was Joe Fredericks, who was known to his fellow inmates and his victims as "Roger". That name fit better. "Roger" is an old English slang term for molesting, and that's what Joseph Roger Fredericks did, as often as he could. Even in death, he's remembered by Oak Ridge staff and patients as a rat, a weasel, a slimy scavenger.

Fredericks had attacked dozens of children and was locked up for almost thirty years in various mental institutions before he even had a criminal record. When the police picked him up, there was nothing on file, no known history of perversion. "Slipped through the cracks" suggests there was a floor, something of substance that Fredericks avoided. Fredericks' keepers, who use that phrase quite often, are much too generous to themselves. If there has ever been a completely evil man in Oak Ridge, someone without any qualities that made him worth keeping alive, it was Roger Fredericks. Maybe he came by his evil honestly, maybe the system that had him in its clutches from the day he was born to the day he died should be blamed for creating him. After all, Roger Fredericks was never a free man. But thousands of other people rise out of rotten childhoods and don't become child rapists. Maybe it was in Roger's lousy genes.

Fredericks was born in 1943, the eleventh of thirteen bastard children of an illiterate, borderline mentally retarded mother. She never played a part in Fredericks' life, and her nurturing qualities seem to have ended at conception. Roger's father's identity is unknown. He may have been an alcoholic or a rapist. Fredericks was born into one of the worst clans in the poverty pockets of the Ottawa Valley, always in trouble with Welfare, the Children's Aid Society and the law.

He spent his youth in foster homes and orphanages run by nuns. Shortly after he learned to walk, he began molesting other children.

In 1954, at the age of eleven, Fredericks finished his formal education. He had been expelled from Grade 3. The nuns had given up on him and the Childrens' Aid had run out of foster homes. Institutions were the only option left. He was sent to the Rideau Regional Centre in Smith Falls, a facility for troubled and mentally handicapped children. Four of his sisters were waiting for him there. When he was sixteen, he escaped from the Rideau Centre and raped a little girl. His next stop was Oak Ridge.

Attendants usually coerced child molesters into being informers, since they were already at the bottom of the Oak Ridge hierarchy. Fredericks was one of two "rats" on B-Ward who snuck around picking up information on other patients, morsels they could sell to the attendants for cigarettes, gum and little favours.

Four years after he arrived at Oak Ridge, Fredericks tried to rape Krueger.

"He got me down in the washroom of the old recreation centre. I was going to the toilet. He said 'Let's do it' and I said, 'No fucking way'. He said 'We're gonna do it'. At that time, a strapping guy came in and saw Fredericks standing over me and me on the floor. He bounced Fredericks off two walls and the ceiling. Then another friend of mine joined in and finished Fredericks off."

Six years after Fredericks arrived, he was given a step toward freedom. In 1963, he was transferred to the Penetanguishene regional psychiatric hospital, but he didn't stay there long. Only a few days after the move, Fredericks escaped and headed to Toronto. Before he had even got out of Penetanguishene, he had robbed a boy of his wind breaker at knifepoint and tried to sodomise him. Within two days of his escape, Fredericks attacked two more boys in Toronto and fondled a six-year-old girl. The girl's mother discovered him molesting the child in the elevator of her apartment building.

She beat the little man to unconsciousness and then called the police. He was returned to Penetanguishene but was never charged because no one expected him to be released again.

Fredericks wanted to get out of Oak Ridge even more than he wanted to rape people smaller than him. Several times, he volunteered to be castrated but the hospital has never performed that surgery. In 1977, he tried to tear out his own testicles with a spoon. Dr. Barker tried many treatments on Roger. He was an eager volunteer for LSD, but he had trouble finding patients who would agree to be his "guides". They were afraid he would become violent and try to bugger them. He was also given liquor in controlled experiments that were supposed to unlock his real feelings. Sodium amytal, the mythical truth serum of World War II, apparently only generated more bravado and lies. In 1975, on amytal, he blamed his wretched existence on "the world, the hospital, doctors and staff. Never during the whole interview was there a slight bit of remorse for being one of the most disliked and distrusted people in this hospital. Fredericks is void of feelings for anyone and the sexual feelings and pity for himself are the only emotions he feels," according to a staff report.

An attendant who saw Fredericks in the therapeutic community's punishment (MAP) program says Fredericks was brutalized by staff and fellow patients: "They would truss him, tie him like a turkey and drop him on the floor. The other patients hated his guts, and they took it out on him in MAP. It was a good thing for him when they stopped the MAP program."

In his own brief autobiography, written when he was just about to leave Oak Ridge, Fredericks had nothing good to say about Oak Ridge: "The only thing they did was medicate me, tranquillize me. That was fine then because I wasn't pointing out things that were wrong, which they call undermining the system. Psychiatrists don't want to deal with psychopaths because they are hard to deal with. It's easier to give someone a pill."

Between "therapy" sessions, Fredericks worked in the upholstery shop. He fantasized about going into business for himself when he got out of Oak Ridge. He also took some courses and got his Grade 8 diploma.

In 1980, Fredericks was transferred, despite warnings from some patients and staff. At the end of his stay, he was on Ward 04, doing fairly well, with a radio, a TV, and, finally, a few friends. It was probably the first time in twenty-two years that Fredericks was fitting into the institution. When the therapeutic community collapsed, the tighter security helped Fredericks avoid the beatings he had received so often. It also cut down on his opportunities for sex, but he was included in a few of the homosexual rings and secret societies that patients were starting to use to keep boredom at bay.

He was sent to St. Thomas Psychiatric Hospital, where he raped a twenty-three-year-old female patient who had the mental development of a small child. The St. Thomas hospital staff loaded him into a car and shipped him to Oak Ridge. Staff in Penetanguishene weren't glad to see him, and almost immediately began planning to get him out of their institution.

The only way to relieve themselves of Fredericks was to send him to another hospital. Staff at Penetanguishene decided to get rid of him in 1983, even though there was no doubt among Oak Ridge patients and staff that Fredericks would rape again. His destination was the Kingston Psychiatric Hospital. Oak Ridge's senior medical officials made it clear to their Kingston colleagues they never wanted to see Fredericks again. If he was to be held in maximum security custody, they wrote, the next time it should be in a penitentiary.

No one in Penetanguishene lost any bets about Fredericks' future. He quickly fulfilled their expectations. Only few weeks passed before Fredericks "eloped", raped a ten-year-old boy and abducted a fifteen-year-old girl at knifepoint. She was rescued by her father. At this point, he had no criminal record, and the Crown Attorney who prosecuted the case didn't know Fredericks was a life-long deviant who preyed on kids. He was treated as a first offender and sentenced to twenty-two months in prison. After serving ten months, he was automatically given parole to a halfway house in Ottawa. It was the first time he had lived in a real house, outside of an institution, since he was eleven. He was supposed to be treated for his sexual deviances, but there was a waiting list. Fredericks couldn't wait.

On his first trip alone from the halfway house, he raped the eleven-year-old son of Swedish diplomat who was fishing in an Ottawa. Fredericks found the boy while he was walking the halfway house's German Shepherd dog. Fredericks threatened to let the dog attack the child if he didn't follow him into the woods and keep quiet.

This attack could have put Fredericks away for life as a dangerous offender, but prosecutors failed because the boy's family quickly returned to Sweden and wouldn't come back for a trial. Fredericks plea bargained for a five-year term. With no witness, the prosecution was lucky to get that.

After three years in jail, he was back on the street again, living in Exodus Link, a Toronto halfway house. Fredericks was supposed to start a drug treatment that would eliminate his sex drive, a type of chemical castration. However, when another halfway house inmate raped and killed a Toronto woman in 1987, a politically-motivated order by the federal solicitor general came down that all sex offenders in the city's halfway houses were to be shipped back to prison. There, in a state of rage, Fredericks waited until the government had to release him, twenty four days later, in March, 1988. When Fredericks got out, he reneged on the drug castration plan. He wasn't welcome in Toronto's halfway houses, so he moved to Brampton.

For the first time in his life, Fredericks had a few real jobs, mostly labouring and cooking in fast food restaurants. Inspired by author Roger Caron, whose book *Go-Boy!* was a best seller in the early 1980s, Roger tried to cash in on his years of being locked up.

Two weeks before he achieved grim fame by committing murder, Fredericks visited Philip Pocock school in Etobicoke as a volunteer for the John Howard Society of Metro Toronto. He was part of a "scared straight" program that was supposed to convince teens to stay out of trouble. Earlier that spring, Fredericks had visited other schools and groups of students had come to a John Howard Society meeting to hear him speak. He was accompanied on the school visits by a probation officer, even though one of the terms of his parole was that he had to stay away from anyone under sixteen. After one session, he took the fifteen-year-old son of a John Howard Society worker to a bar and bought him a few beers. He would lie to the kids, telling them that he had been out for eight years, after serving time for murder. Fredericks also worked as a sort of babysitter in John Howard Society office, looking after the children of other convicts.

On Friday, 17 June, 1988, Fredericks kidnapped eleven-year-old Christopher Stephenson from Shopper's World mall in Brampton. After a night of sexual assaults, he murdered the young boy and left his body in the woods near the mall.

Caught within hours, Fredericks was found sane and convicted of first degree murder. Judge Thomas Granger rejected Frederick's lawyer's plea that Fredericks should be sent to a super-protective custody wing at Kingston Penitentiary.

Granger, in effect, sentenced Fredericks to death. In a prison upholstery shop, Fredericks was murdered with a pair of upholstery shears on 3 January, 1992. He was forty-nine-years-old.

Daniel Poulin, his murderer, pleaded guilty to manslaughter. At Poulin's trial, even the prosecutor, the representative of the victim and society, had nothing good to say about Fredericks. He described Roger as "one of the most despised men in Canada". Poulin claimed he had carried out prison justice for Fredericks' crimes. Poulin was sentenced to ten years, concurrent to the time he was already serving. In effect, he didn't have to spend an extra day in jail for killing Fredericks.

Despite these grotesque failures, de-institutionalization continued at Oak Ridge thorough the 1980s. David Michael Krueger, now middle-aged and superbly educated in the intricacies of social and mental manipulation, was considered by "progressive" social workers and psychiatrists to be a prime candidate for release. Despite warnings from some of the people who knew him best, by the late 1980s, Krueger was being rushed out the door of Oak Ridge.

THE BROTHERHOODS

Through the 1980s, the newspapers were loaded with stories about Fredericks, Gillis, and lesser-known Oak Ridge alumni who had been released and screwed up. The institution's own research department was busy cranking out academic papers showing that many of the psychopaths who had be treated in the therapeutic community experiments could barely wait for the chance to kill again. Pedophiles, like the psychopathic killers, were described in the new academic papers as untreatable, yet killers and child molesters were leaving Penetanguishene even faster than they had in the days of the therapeutic community. Some of the patients who passed through Oak Ridge had controllable illnesses like schizophrenia and manic depression, which respond very well to medications. Many more were people whose release was a gamble with public safety. Woodcock fell into that category.

With Woodcock, the warning signs of more homicide were always there, and the people who knew him best saw them fairly easily. For nearly twenty years, however, he had a spotless record in the institution. The pressure was building to let him out. Woodcock had served a very long stretch of time, as much as he would have spent in prison for the same crimes. Even if he hadn't been given parole, he would have, at least, been moved out of a maximum security prison to a more comfortable institution after two decades of good behaviour.

In the mid-1970s, Woodcock hit a bump in the road that, temporarily, blotted his unsoiled record. This turned out to be fortunate for children and small adults on the outside. In the midst of the therapeutic community, while he was clipping along as one of the psychopathic lords of his ward, Woodcock hatched an idea. He would recreate the Winchester Heights Gang, the other patients would recognize him as their leader, and they would pay him tribute in the currency of Oak Ridge. The Winchester Heights Gang name wouldn't do, of course. He needed something a little more ominous. Woodcock settled on the name "The Brotherhood". This organization couldn't be confined to Oak Ridge. It had to have power outside the institution, powerful friends who could do harm to the families of inmates who didn't co-operate, and who could help patients when they were released.

The Brotherhood started slowly. Woodcock knew which patients were more likely to buy into the fantasy. One at a time, he recruited members among the more ill people on his ward. Eventually, the fantasy started coming true: Woodcock, for the first time in his life, was the leader of a full-fledged conspiracy. Of course, it was too good to last. The problem with The Brotherhood was that it was no democracy, and there was nothing in it for Woodcock's followers. Unlike a chain letter, where a few people benefit at the expense of the rest of the dupes, The Brotherhood had only one beneficiary. Woodcock was the supreme leader, and everyone initiated into the organization had to perform fellatio on him. They also gave Woodcock cash and cigarettes, along with the sex. It couldn't last forever. On Tuesday, 26 August, 1975, staff found out about the Brotherhood. Woodcock was caught only a few weeks after he'd told Dr. Maier that he was ready to "go all the way" on LSD and get to the demons inside him.

Fred West, an impressionable new arrival on G Ward, where Woodcock held sway over lowlifes like Fredericks, was the first to be conned into believing that Woodcock had powerful links to sinister forces. West did his brotherly duty, but Woodcock had already scared him with so many stories about the reach of The Brotherhood that West spent weeks terrified that Woodcock would turn on him and would get other people in The Brotherhood to West's family. Staff realized that something was going on, but they couldn't get panic-stricken West to rat on Woodcock. At first, West just said he wanted to go back to Guelph Reformatory. Then, under Sodium Amytal, West talked. Confronted with West's information, Woodcock admitted everything about The Brotherhood, and was sent to the MAP program to be straightened out.

Once Woodcock was caught, many of the other inmates who had been conned into believing that he was all-powerful soon realized they had been duped. They spoke darkly about getting even. Dr. Maier wrote to his superiors that "Peter may be assaulted or even murdered by one of the patients." Moreover, Dr. Maier said, Woodcock's chances of release from Oak Ridge were now "Null and void. I do not believe he will receive a recommendation to leave this hospital. My concern is that he will all too clearly see this understanding himself. He has become overnight a real suicide risk. We of course will take every precaution possible to secure his life in this regard, too.

"While the possibility of a 'Brotherhood' is little more than a fantasy, Peter's position in our Unit has definitely changed and it will be months if not years before we can relax our security in regard to his welfare."

Dr. Maier would not be the last therapist to be betrayed by Krueger. Anyone who believed he was trustworthy then, or believes he's improved now, has never understood that solid core of vicious fantasy that lies at the centre of Krueger. It is unshakable. It got Peter Woodcock through his adolescence and it gets David Michael Krueger through every day at Oak Ridge. I've seen it many times. Very gently, he has tried to seduce me into The Brotherhood, dropping little hints, pretending he's telling me about fantasies of the past. I'm sure, too, that, in his mind, I am already part of it.

More than twenty years after The Brotherhood conspiracy made it obvious to Dr. Maier that Woodcock values his dark fantasies more than anything else, including freedom, Krueger called my home to chat, mostly about the weather. Talk turned to Toronto and its east-end Rouge River Valley, which Krueger said he wanted to see preserved "as an oasis in the city."

"The kids need a place to play," he said.

I reminded Krueger that, with people like him around, many people think twice about letting their kids out of their sight, let alone allowing them to go to a wilderness area in Toronto.

"Predators need a place to play, too," he said with a chuckle. Then he added, "if you can't make fun of yourself, who can you make fun of?"

After nearly forty years, all those experimental treatments, all that time locked up, all of the energy that has gone into trying to rehabilitate him, all of the trusts that he's created and broken, that central core of evil was still there, still so strong. Even during the 1970s, when the therapeutic community seemed to hold out so much hope for Woodcock, there was strong opposition to him ever being released. J. P. Rickaby, a Toronto deputy Crown attorney, had a plan to charge Woodcock for the Mallette and Morris murders if he was set free. Since there is no statute of limitations for murder in Canada, that threat still hangs over Krueger, though, with the insanity verdict in the Carole Voyce murder as a precedent, a good lawyer should be able to win an acquittal. Still, he worries about those old charges and mentions them every few months.

The Brotherhood really should have been no surprise. In July, 1973, Woodcock had been sent to the Queen Street psychiatric hospital in Toronto for assessment. The fact that he was in the city leaked out to the media, and the institution began fielding threatening phone calls. While Krueger blames this for his return to Oak Ridge, the real reason lies in the negative assessment of Queen Street staff: two of the six therapists who studied him were in favour of slowly preparing him for release, one was lukewarm to the idea, while the rest realized that he continued to be a danger to children. Two months later, he was at Toronto's Clarke Institute for more interviews. This time, one of the psychiatrists was a doctor who had seen Woodcock in 1957, in the weeks just after his arrest. This psychiatrist, along with his colleagues, blackballed any chance of Woodcock's release.

All of these studies showed that Woodcock could maintain a mask of sanity while he was institutionalized in Oak Ridge, but once things around him changed, he reverted back to his fantasy life and, eventually, at least partly lost touch with reality. The tests showed "there is a psychotic core deeply imbedded in his personality ... testing reveals a capacity for poor reality testing which can occur under situations of stress with the possibility of explosive and aggressive behaviour."

There were, however, factors working for Krueger's release. Governments wanted to "de-institutionalize" long-term patients to save money and to give them the freedom that many rights activists demanded. The public may say it wants dangerous people like Krueger locked away forever, but taxpayers don't want to pay the cost of lifelong incarceration or for follow-up treatment for those patients who are released on medication. We're a cheap, mean society in many ways. Patients who are treatable are freed with a prescription and sent to live in poverty, without the help they relied on when they were in an institution. They don't fit into society. The medication they take usually has nasty side effects. They stop taking it, commit a crime or become a nuisance, are arrested and returned to the institution, where the cycle begins again. Many psychiatric patients need attention that can come only from living with caring families or in housing that combines medical treatment and life in the outside world.

Perhaps the most interesting activist for the destruction of Oak Ridge is Randy Pritchard, an Ottawa Valley man who was picked up in Ottawa with the makings of a bomb that he planned to throw into the House of Commons from the visitors' gallery. He spent five months in Oak Ridge before being set free to begin a campaign against the institution. Since then, he has levied charges ranging from murder and brutality to the keeping of unmarked graves on the hospital's grounds. None of the charges have been substantiated, although police have investigated them. Through the years, Pritchard lost support among other activists, but for nearly a decade, he caused trouble for Oak Ridge and was banned from the hospital's grounds. He says much of his anger comes from the way he was treated in the institution:

"On my very first day, they stripped me naked at the end of a corridor and marched me down to the showers to delouse me. Then they took me to a cell with a concrete bunk. I sat dripping on the bunk. Five hours later, they gave me a gown. I was kept in the cell for three days before I was allowed out. After two weeks, I was transferred to a treatment ward. At the time, they had a committee system, with patients treating patients. We decided what kind of drugs would be prescribed to new patients, the dosages and how often they would be taken. The psychiatrists would just sign the prescriptions.

"Our committees would deal with the hundreds of petty rules. In there, if someone showed anger, they ended up in a cell called a safe room with a concrete bunk. If they got sad, the attendants would say that they couldn't predict what the patients would do, and into the safe room they would go. There's no treatment at Oak Ridge. All you get is polished liars who know what to say to get more privileges and eventually get transferred out of there."

It still is a tough place: even in the 1990s, when critics howled for the closure of Oak Ridge, guards felt so sure of their power that they could hand the clinical files of inmates to favoured reporters and taunt patients. Robert Keiling, a Prairie wheat farmer who became obsessed with Anne Murray, was locked up in Oak Ridge for observation after one of his attempts to visit the singer. Guards hummed Murray's signature tune "Snowbird" as they walked by his cell.

Randy Pritchard's beliefs about the failure of Oak Ridge treatment programs were shared by the new breed of psychologists who had taken charge in the wake of the therapeutic community. The Oak Ridge research staff issued a flurry of academic papers saying that the recidivism rate for the psychopaths who had been through the therapeutic community was actually higher than for psychopaths who hadn't been part of the experiment. Somehow, that message wasn't getting to the review board or to policy setters. At the same time that it was becoming clear that there was no known treatment for psychopaths that caused them to become any less dangerous, people like Gillis, Fredericks and Krueger were being transferred out of Oak Ridge to institutions where they were given day passes and prepared for life in the outside world. The science just didn't fit with the conventional wisdom of the time, which was leaning more towards the individual rights of patients to release, rather than to the collective rights of society to be protected. It was no coincidence that this policy was also, at least on the surface, cheaper than providing humane, decent long-term care in a place secure enough to keep psychopaths from escaping.

There was always a struggle between factions, both inside and outside of Oak Ridge, over whether the goal of the hospital should be to treat and release inmates, or to simply house them as a way of protecting society. In 1989, a small civil wedding ceremony, the first one held inside Oak Ridge, caused sparring matches between advocates of a strict security system and those who believed in rehabilitation. Garry Lenehan, the leader of the nurses' union at Oak Ridge, called the wedding "frills and thrills at taxpayers' expense", while the lawyer for the inmate groom wrote in the Penetanguishene newspaper that "the overall benefit to the government is represented by an individual being discharged from the hospital much quicker". Since Oak Ridge has no conjugal facilities, the honeymoon had to wait. The groom did, however, leave the institution soon afterwards.

Oak Ridge struggled to keep up with society in other ways: the grey and institutional green interior was fixed up, fake plants were hung on some wards, and a new recreation centre was built to diffuse criticism that Oak Ridge was a prison, not a hospital; female security staff were hired in 1983; patient advocates came into the institution, at government expense, soon afterwards. The growing litigiousness of society, coupled with the passing of the Charter of Rights and Freedoms, meant many Oak Ridge patients became plaintiffs in lawsuits against the institution and its staff. Some of these legal actions succeeded: patients are no longer forced to take medication, thanks to one court ruling. Nor do they have to work.

In 1982, staff at St. Thomas Psychiatric Hospital, which ran a long-term program to prepare Oak Ridge inmates and other dangerous psychiatric patients for release, examined Krueger. The psychiatrists didn't like what they saw:

"It is recommended that Peter not be transferred to St. Thomas Psychiatric Hospital, Medium Security, at this time. It is believed that there remains a substantial risk of further child molestation. This is based on a number of factors. One is the relatively short period of time that Peter's behaviour was exemplary at Penetang. The second is his current mental state, his inability to express emotions is outstanding. His need for emotional expression and over people in social and sexual situations is worrisome. The psychological test data show affective over control with the possibility of sudden unpredictable outbursts, egocentricity, a poor self-concept, distrust of others, and a view of the world as a threatening and dangerous place."

At Oak Ridge, Krueger became a model inmate again as memories of The Brotherhood faded. Within a few years, the patients who had been duped had either been transferred out of Oak Ridge or had forgotten about what had happened. Staff began believing the scheme was just a slip-up. Krueger made himself useful. He ran a current events class and sessions on translating hospital jargon for new inmates. By 1984, he had been locked up for twenty-seven-years. Some of Krueger's caretakers inside the mental health system began to have ethical problems about incarcerating someone who had been found not guilty for a longer period than if a jury had ruled he was guilty. They had to balance this quandary with the threat that Krueger posed to the public, and to himself because of his inability to function in the outside world.

* * *

In 1985, Krueger was sent to the Royal Ottawa Hospital for assessment by Dr. John Bradford, who would later do the analysis of serial killer Paul Bernardo. Bradford found no change in Krueger's level of dangerousness since the St. Thomas examination. His tests showed "sadistic heterosexual pedophilic responses". Still, Oak Ridge staff wanted Krueger to begin a program in a medium security hospital to learn the life skills he would need to live on the outside. In August, 1986, despite the opposition of St. Thomas staff, Krueger was shipped there. Krueger hated St. Thomas from the time he arrived. At first, he tried to make the administrators of the hospital happy by participating in group therapy sessions and by sucking up to them. When other patients criticised him, however, Krueger became angry and began plotting ways to get even with his fellow inmates and the staff. Within a few weeks, he was disliked by the healthier patients and many of the therapists. Krueger began looking for supporters among the duller people on his ward.

Since St. Thomas didn't know him very well, Krueger could do things that staff at Oak Ridge quickly would have jumped on. For instance, who would care if a pedophile psychiatric patient sent away for a department store catalogue? It's not an obvious problem until you open the kid's clothing pages and see the underwear ads. They're a magnet for child molesters. At Oak Ridge, Krueger used to clip the pictures and hide them in the back of his radio, until he was caught. At St. Thomas, he told staff he would be helped if he could read magazine articles about child abuse. They saw it as uplifting literature. To him, it was pornography.

Then, as he retreated deeper into his diamond-hard world of gangs and murder, he revived The Brotherhood. His first initiate was a rather large man who was quickly pressed into service as a bodyguard. Unfortunately, Krueger's big friend wasn't the silent type. He blathered to other inmates about the Brotherhood, how it could settle scores with them, whether they were in the hospital or on the outside. At the same time, Krueger recruited more patients into the fraternity and began planning an escape by taking staff members as hostages. Krueger had also fallen in love with another man on the ward, and, to get at him, Krueger cut the wire from a lamp, stripped the positive and negative lines to make crude electrodes, and waited for the chance to lunge at his victim and zap him into unconsciousness. Word of all of these plots reached St. Thomas' staff. Attendants yanked Krueger out of his room and hauled him in front of a tribunal of psychiatrists and ward staffs. Within hours, Krueger was on his way back to Penetanguishene. Staff at St. Thomas, who now fully realized how dangerous Krueger is, sent a blizzard of memos through the psychiatric system declaring that Krueger must never be let out, and should be watched carefully. They wanted him locked away for life in maximum security. Instead, his stay at Oak Ridge would be three years.

* * *

When he arrived back at Oak Ridge, Krueger was contrite. He said he had staged The Brotherhood at St. Thomas so that he could be returned to Penetanguishene, his home. Some of the staff seem to have been flattered. There was none of the punishment that came after the first Brotherhood incident. Instead, he was given most of his old privileges back and was sent to work in the kitchen. He began to take university courses in English and the philosophy of science. Within a year, he was, again, being described as a model inmate.

Still, he was not thrilled to be back. He became depressed, telling staff that he was afraid that he would die or go blind soon. An image of his coffin being lowered into the ground seemed to stick in his mind. It troubled him that there would be no mourners at his funeral. He tried to cloak the self-pity in a shroud of fake remorse for his victims.

The wheels of the psychiatric system continued to turn. In December, 1988, a Dr. Heasman met Krueger for the first time. He seems to have found Krueger intriguing. They had a fairly long chat, long enough for Dr. Heasman, who seems to be a good judge of character, to realize that Krueger hides a very vicious entity behind his polite and fawning exterior. Krueger warmed up to Dr. Heasman. He talked in circles, often contradicting himself. He said he was ready to begin down "the long rehabilitation road", yet he knew that he could never live in the outside world. He said he did not want to leave Oak Ridge, that if he did, he would "move on and kill". Krueger admitted that scenes of semi-clad children on television were a turn-on for him, but promised to repress those feelings. He offered to take medication that would squelch his sex drive.

On his ward, Krueger was busy with life skills training and stress management. He told staff that he still had his vicious urges, but he had developed the self-control to seek help if they began to be a problem. Through the next year, Krueger's lawyers began looking for psychologists and psychiatrists who would support his desire to move out of Oak Ridge. That was their job. On the other side, the Crown attorney had a responsibility to bring evidence to the Lieutenant-Governor's Board of Review from psychiatrists who held contrary views, if there were any. The Crown would fulfil that obligation. In the middle was the board: two psychiatrists, a lawyer, a representative of the public, and a retired Supreme Court justice. It would be up to them to decide whether Krueger would have a shot at freedom.

Dr. Stephen Hucker, one of the province's top psychiatrists, had conducted a study on Oak Ridge that had recommended the place be closed. He was no friend of the Penetanguishene institution, slamming it for its bleak surroundings, undertrained staff and lousy treatment. Yet, after meeting Krueger, reading his file, and questioning him about his fantasy life, he wasn't eager to let Krueger leave Oak Ridge. This was obviously a dangerous man who needed to be kept tightly locked away, he told the review board:

"His pattern of offenses before his arrest and subsequent acquittal by reason of insanity reflect serious anomalous sexual arousal patterns of a sadistic pedophilic kind. Abnormal erotic preferences are relatively fixed and this view is essentially supported in this case by laboratory tests involving physiological measures of his sexual arousal. The question is whether or not Mr. Krueger would act out this preference again. In my opinion, this is still a possibility even after many years of incarceration and there has, of course, been repeated concern or suspicion over the years about continued inappropriate sexual behaviour. Were he to be given a sex drive reducing medication, the risk MIGHT be lessened but this could not be guaranteed.

"In addition to his sexual anomalies, Mr. Krueger has a schizotypal personality disorder. In other words, despite the passage of time and the possible effects of therapy, he is still an odd man in his thoughts and behaviour. The possibility of frank psychotic regression or liability to poor judgement is still present. I have serious questions about his explanation of his most recent transfer back from St. Thomas as it seems to follow the long-standing pattern of preoccupation with "brotherhoods" and subversive activity. Even if one chooses to believe his own account that it was a ruse to expedite his removal back to Oak Ridge, it is a plan reflecting very questionable judgement and insight into his situation. If he had, as I have said I am inclined to believe, and as did the staff at St. Thomas, a more malignant intent, then placement in a setting of less than maximum security would be inappropriate.

"Consequently, though I am cognizant of the fact that Mr. Krueger has already spent a very long period of time in detention and there are humanitarian concerns over deterioration of his vision and hearing, I am not able to recommend that Mr. Krueger be managed in a less secure environment at this time."

Three other clinicians sent reports to the review board saying Krueger was ready to be moved out of Oak Ridge. His lawyer proposed that Krueger take a four-month treatment programme for sex offenders at the Clarke Institute Toronto and then be sent to Brockville. They also wanted Krueger to be given female hormones that would depress his sex drive by "chemically castrating" him. Neither happened. The Clarke didn't accept murderers into its program, and the androgyny drugs were never given to Krueger. He was shipped to Brockville as-is.

The review board seemed to think that Brockville could hold Krueger, and that he wouldn't outwit the institution's administration:

"In the hearing today it was clear that no one can say that this patient is no longer a risk to the public should he be released on the streets. That, however, is not the question that faces the Board today. The question which faces the Board is, can he be equally well treated in a medium secure institution, and can he be as safely treated in a medium security institution as he would be in a maximum security institution? All the psychiatric tests made, and the psychological testing, indicates that this patient is not an elopement risk. The majority of the evidence indicates that he can be safely kept in a medium secure institution. The majority of the evidence, however, indicates that this patient might benefit by a change in the hospital in which he is kept, even though the main treatment suggested at this time is life skills, and these skills are now being emphasized at the Mental Health Centre, Penetanguishene, Oak Ridge Division.

"In examining the evidence of the Consultant, and the Hospital, it becomes clear that they are of the opinion that this patient has not recovered from his mental illness at this time, and in that there is a consensus of agreement. It also become clear from the evidence of Dr. Hucker, that he is of the opinion that the actions of the patient at the St. Thomas Psychiatric Hospital in 1986 were malignant rather than explainable as the patient does explain them.

"This Board, however, finds itself convinced by the vast majority of the evidence before it that this patient can be treated in a medium secure hospital equally safely as he could in the Mental Health Centre, Penetanguishene. We are further convinced that this patient can receive at least as good treatment in a medium secure institution as he is receiving at this Hospital.

"The sum total of the evidence leaves us with the opinion that it is in the best interest of this patient, as well as to the public at large, that he be treated in a medium secure hospital and that the patient at that time be given an androgen blocking agent."

The decision was signed "The Honourable Donald R. Morand, Q.C., Alternate Chairman, the Lieutenant Governor's Board of Review."

Oak Ridge staff knew better. They issued one last warning, this time to Brockville staff. It was included in Krueger's discharge summary.

"The hospital's recommendation to the Board in December of 1988 was that there be no change in the warrant. It is felt that Mr. Krueger continues to have deviant sexual thoughts and fantasies and due to his coldness and lack of skills and his in-depth fantasy life, that he would be dangerous to younger members of society. In fairness to Mr. Krueger, we indicated that we felt it was unclear what point in time, or under what circumstances, a recommendation for a move would ever be made. Nevertheless, we continued to encourage him to participate in all levels of programming and to make full use of these.

"Given that Mr. Krueger has received a recommendation by the Lieutenant-Governor's Board of Review to move to the Brockville Psychiatric Hospital, we must comply.

"We recommend strongly that Mr. Krueger be well supervised around the hospital and on the grounds and that he be involved intensively in various forms of programs related to moral value and beliefs training as well as life skills programming to focus on deinstitutionalization rather than reintegration into society."

This warning, by Oak Ridge chief psychiatrist Russell Fleming, and by unit director Brenda Knight, is one of the most astute summaries of Krueger's dangerousness that exists in his file. Not only, in three short paragraphs, did they describe his personality, but they even forecast the place, and, to an extent, the victim, of his next murder.

KNIGHT OF THE
PRAETORIAN GUARD

The Ottawa neighbourhood of New Edinburgh is the kind of place where most Canadians would like to live. The shady streets are clean and safe. The Rideau River, fringed with parks and spanned by a lovely antique bridge, runs along the edge of the neighbourhood. There's a strong sense of community, which shows itself in the support that New Edinburghers give to their churches and schools.

It has the feeling, like most of Ottawa, of being a small town. For most of its history, it was, indeed, a village on its own, until the capital grew northeastward to meet it. Streets are named after New Edinburgh's founders, who built comfortable stone houses on the east side of the Rideau, near where it joins the Ottawa River, in the 1840s. Back then, Ottawa was a rough little lumbering village called Bytown, a place that few decent people wanted to live in. The first settlers of New Edinburgh sought a quiet, respectable life, so they shunned the shanties, the taverns and the whorehouses of Bytown and built sensible little houses in their own village.

They were blessed with some natural splendour. The Rideau River splits in two and empties into the Ottawa River by tumbling over a fifteen-metre cliff. The falls look like two curtains (which, in French, are rideau). At Confederation, the grandest house in the village, Rideau Hall, was leased by the government to be the headquarters of the Governor General. A few years later, the old stone mansion, along with its eighty-five acres, was purchased outright. This estate marks the eastern boundary of the community. In the northwest corner, near the gates to Rideau Hall, is the Prime Minister's mansion at 24 Sussex Drive. The massive, imposing French embassy fills the space between 24 Sussex and the Rideau Falls.

Most of the houses in New Edinburgh aren't nearly so grand. For years, Margaret Trudeau has lived in a Victorian house a few blocks from the Prime Minister's residence. Like most other New Edinburgh homes, her house is modest, with a good-sized backyard, and easy access to the local parks. New Edinburgh's streets have a mixture of stone, brick and wood houses, mostly two or three-bedroom. Some have been renovated, but most are still just well-kept turn-of-the century homes that would fit into any older city neighbourhood in Canada.

MacKay Street runs along the edge of the Rideau Hall estate, connecting to Sussex Drive less than a block from the Prime Minister's house. The Governor General's residence is enclosed by a handsome wrought-iron fence. On the lawns of Government House, unreconstructed colonials still play cricket in the summer. On summer weekends, bands and orchestras give free concerts. People take tours of the Rideau Hall greenhouses, walk the grounds, and, in the winter, go to skating parties hosted by the Governor General. On the west side of the street, Bruce Hamill grew up in a little white-framed house, set back from the street. It's an ugly place, made more-so by the strange placement of the house's front windows. The house is pinched in between a much nicer home to the north and a duplex to the south. Most of the front yard is a driveway gravelled in black mine slag.

The house backs on to a laneway. These little roads run behind most New Edinburgh houses. They give the local kids a safe place to learn how to ride their bikes and are easy shortcuts through the neighbourhood. Kitty-corner to the back of the Hamill house is a ninety-year-old school. Bruce Hamill is one of its less-successful graduates, and he chose it to be the scene of his first murder.

Bruce Waldemar Charles Hamill was born 27 November, 1956. His mother was thirty-two, his father forty-seven. Fairly quickly, the Hamills realized Bruce had behavioral problems. He was born with a temporal lobe abnormality, which shows up on EEG and CAT scans. His right temporal lobe has atrophied, causing impulsive and aggressive behaviour that comes out in brief bursts of incredibly violent rages.

Through his childhood and teen years, Wally and Gertrude Hamill sheltered Bruce and tried to pretend that there was nothing seriously wrong with him. If he got into trouble, they blamed his friends. If he was in a fight, it was never his fault. They knew that Bruce had mental problems, and had found a psychiatrist for him, but the Hamill family did not believe he was dangerous. Sometimes, he had violent fits at home and lashed out at the family, but they told themselves his anger was just part of life for a young man who had trouble fitting in.

Bruce's emotional problems were just part of the strange dynamics of the Hamill household. Gertrude Hamill liked to believe that the world mistreated her entire family. She rose to the task of protecting her son from the outside world, even telling him not to take pills prescribed by his psychiatrist, but she, too, had trouble coping with reality. Gertrude Hamill became a life-long victim, blaming the government, the city, her neighbours, and any other outsiders who crossed her, for her troubles. Her son saw himself as her protector.

As a teenager, Bruce's rages became more frequent. By Grade 10, he was buying street drugs from the dealers in downtown Ottawa. He had a few odd jobs, and, when he turned eighteen, spent a summer in the militia. There, he met Robert Poulin, another violent, troubled kid who would become a killer. At Petawawa, Terry Chisamore shared a tent with Hamill and Robert Poulin. Chisamore says Poulin was gung-ho, but Hamill mostly moped around. For two weeks, they did manouevers, day and night, in the pine forests surrounding the Petawawa base. Poulin was a model recruit, thrilled by the guns and the jeeps. He slept with his rifle by his side, while, across the tent, Hamill lay, miserable and homesick, among his gear. Hamill told Chisamore that enthusiasts like Poulin were "fanatics and weirdos."

Hamill and Poulin came to blows one day while on patrol. Poulin was enraged that Hamill's mess tin was filthy. Word had also spread among the men of the unit that Hamill was homosexual, and Poulin had become worried that other soldiers would think he, too, was gay.

"I got sick, and a lot of us went home sick," Hamill later told writer Chris Cobb. "There's a lot of things you have to do and it's just ridiculous and you have to do it because it's the army."

The better soldiers, like Poulin, applied to be members of the security unit that guarded the 1976 Montreal Olympics. In the meantime, an elite group, including Poulin, created a secret commando unit that trained in an Ottawa gym. Through the fall, Poulin was falling apart. In a rage, classmate, he raped and a schoolmate, Kim Rabot, and left her body in a basement. A few minutes later, he attacked his theology class at Pius X Highs School, gunning down two more students before shooting himself.

* * *

After his stint in the militia, Hamill became more violent. A few months after he left the army base at Petawawa, Hamill went to visit a homosexual friend. They smoked marijuana and drank until the gay man passed out. Hamill raised a knife over the man's exposed back, then ran the blade along his back, side and stomach. He wondered what it would feel like to plunge the blade in. This time, Hamill stopped himself.

Just after Christmas, he beat a twelve-year-old boy to a pulp because the youth said something that Hamill took to be an insult. And, two weeks before he finally did kill someone, Hamill had gone to Ottawa's Lisgar Street Collegiate at the end of a school day to stab a student who had insulted him three years before. For days, Hamill had worked himself into a rage thinking about what the boy had said to him. The youth couldn't remember Hamill, had no idea why the man chased him around the school yard with a knife, and was lucky to get away alive.

Through those months, Hamill was still seeing his psychiatrist, but in early February, he stopped. Gertrude Hamill told her son that the sessions were a waste of time. There was nothing wrong with Bruce and the rest of the family, she said. So Bruce missed his appointments, stopped taking his pills, and became crazy enough to commit murder.

Hamill's rage finally focused on Betty Wentzlaff, a fifty-eight-year-old cleaning lady. She and her husband George had lived next to the Hamills for twenty-one years and had gone out of their way to be friendly with them. The Wentzlaffes had no children, so they gave some of their time to the Hamills. Gertrude and Wally had invited Betty and George to their 25th anniversary party, and the families often visited each other. Things between the neighbours were fine until Gertrude Hamill decided that she wanted the Wentzlaff house for her daughter. In her mind, the Wentzlaffes had no choice but to sell. When they refused, Gertrude Hamill began building a hatred-filled fantasy world with Betty Wentzlaff at the centre. Bruce watched his mother become fixated on Betty. While she would only complain about Mrs. Wentzlaff, Bruce was willing to act.

On the night of 28 February 1977, Gertrude Hamill called Betty Wentzlaff to ask her, once again, to sell her house to Bruce's sister. During the phone call, Bruce's mother shouted at Wentzlaff. She screamed that the neighbour was being unreasonable, that she wasn't grateful for the friendship she had been shown by the Hamills.

When she set down the phone, Bruce's mother was crying. Bruce decided he would fix the problem. He left the house, saying he was going to see a movie. Walking the streets of the village, along the outer fence of the Governor General's estate, and back towards MacKay Street, Bruce became more enraged. He thought about his mother, who had stayed loyal to him through the bad months. In his mind, Mrs. Wentzlaff became the persecutor of his family. She had deliberately set out to ruin the Hamill family and make his mother unhappy. He decided Betty Wentzlaff had to die.

For four years, Wentzlaff had worked as a part-time cleaner at Chrichton Street School, just behind her house. Hamill followed her to work at about 5 a.m. In the darkness, Betty saw him climbing the fence behind his house and running after her. She tried to get into a side door of the school to escape, but Hamill caught up to her. He stabbed Betty twenty-seven times before scurrying back to his home.

Betty Wentzlaff was found dead about 6:45 a.m. by school superintendent Jean-Guy Charette, just three feet from the back door of the school. Hours later, Charette was still crying in his office when a reporter phoned him.

"She was like a mother to everyone. Even the school children called her Betty," he told a reporter..

That day, the school's administration sent letters to the parents of the ninety-three students at Crighton Street School. The choice of words was interesting:

"Dear Parents,

"As you are quite aware, we have had an unfortunate accident happen to Mrs. Betty Wentzlaff, one of our dear and devoted members of the custodial staff. This has come to us with great surprise and dismay because New Edinburgh is one of the most peaceful areas of our city.

"In case there may be some concern in the neighbourhood, may I stress that this has been and will remain a good place to live and send your children to school. I do trust that you will continue to send your children to school after 8:30 in the morning and be sure to pick them up promptly at dismissal time. Children who have lunch at noon at the school are not allowed to leave during this time.

"Reg Westerman (principal)."

Police were baffled by the Wentzlaff murder. She had no enemies that anyone knew of. The more they learned about Betty Wentzlaff, the angrier and more determined the investigators became.

"It's just senseless," one detective told a local reporter. "How could a guy like that sleep at night, knowing what he has done? He has got to be crazy. He stabbed an old woman like that so many times."

Police quickly ruled out robbery, since Wentzlaff still had a small amount of money in her pocket. There was also no sign of sexual assault. At first, they believed she may have surprised an intruder in the school. There was very little evidence to go on. Ice covered the ground at the murder scene, so there were no footprints.

On Thursday morning, two days after Wentzlaff's murder, while Wally and Gertrude were shopping at the local IGA, police arrested Bruce. Once they had him in handcuffs, they searched the house, finding the knife that had been used to kill Betty. When Bruce's parents arrived home from the store, Bruce had been taken away, but the search was still going on. The police drove Wally and Gertrude to the police station and let them sit with their son in an interrogation room.

"They've charged me with murder," Bruce told his mother. "And I did it."

* * *

Reporters crowded into a press conference later Thursday to learn about Hamill. Staff Superintendent Tom Flanagan told them: "We've recovered a number of things and taken them into our possession."

"Are you still looking for the knife?" a reporter asked.

"No," Flanagan answered. "We are no longer looking for a weapon."

The police praised the people of New Edinburgh for the dozens of tips that investigators received, but were coy about how they had narrowed the search to Bruce Hamill.

"We knocked on virtually every door," Flanagan told reporters. "The whole police force was involved. The lack of evidence and the viciousness of the attack on Mrs. Wentzlaff made it a tough murder that had to be worked on in a very tough way."

Gertrude Hamill was more forthcoming with Kit Collins, an *Ottawa Citizen* reporter who knocked on her door just after noon. Wally Hamill was sitting in the kitchen when Gertrude ushered Collins inside the gloomy home.

"I had a premonition something was wrong," Wally told Collins.

"I didn't," Gertrude said. "Bruce went to a movie Monday night, then went for a pizza on Rideau Street. When he got home, we sat in the living room and ate it while we watched the late show.

"And in the morning, I didn't hear anything. Bruce usually slept until noon when he wasn't working. I woke up about six, the first time, then I got up at eight. Bruce was already up and dressed. We had a half a grapefruit each. Bruce said he had trouble sleeping."

Gertrude said she had no suspicions until she came home from the IGA and found the police rummaging through her house.

"My head feels like it wants to blow, but if that's the way that he's got to get help, okay. But he was getting help in the first place."

That afternoon, the pews of St. Luke's Lutheran Church in New Edinburgh were filled with about a hundred mourners. George Wentzlaff sat with his wife's mother. Six of Betty's brothers and sisters sat nearby. The rest of the mourners were teachers and students from Crichton Street School, where the flag still flew at half mast.

* * *

In the fall of 1978, Hamill was taken to Oak Ridge for assessment. Dr. Russell Fleming interviewed Hamill several times and came to the conclusion that the killer was sane at the time he stabbed Betty Wentzlaff.

Hamill tried to come across as a tough city kid who wouldn't let someone push around his family.

"I believe that if you fight people, they leave you alone. Mrs. Wentzlaff was a low-class, stupid woman who thought she could just push us around," Hamill told Dr. Fleming.

"What did you think about on the night of the murder?" Dr. Fleming asked.

"I thought about killing her. I didn't think about anything else. Like, I didn't think that I would get caught or anything. Afterwards, I was scared like hell. I knew that I did it, but I couldn't realize that I'd done it. Does that make sense? I saw my whole life go in front of me, thinking about the future."

"Your future?" Fleming asked.

"Yes," Hamill replied.

He stared out the window of the Oak Ridge ward sunroom for a few minutes, not saying anything.

"I don't remember what she looked like, even."

Hamill's tough exterior was starting to wear thin. He wanted Dr. Fleming to know why he committed the crime, that he had flipped out dozens of times over the years.

"If something had been done for me, if the medication had been stronger, maybe it wouldn't have happened.

"I guess I have a bad temper. My emotions go nuts on me. I can't go to prison. I wouldn't last a second. People waste away there like in a warehouse. If they send me here, I would work really hard. I'd even let them do surgery. I don't want to go to prison," he said.

* * *

Hamill's trial began Monday, 9 January, in the city's old courthouse. For a little more than a week, psychiatrists would argue over the young man's sanity.

Dr. Selwyn Smith, head of forensic psychiatry at the Royal Ottawa Hospital, the city's main psychiatric institution, testified Mrs. Wentzlaff's murder was premeditated but the reasons behind it were irrational.

He explained how the family was dysfunctional, how Bruce's mother saw herself as a victim, and her son as a protector. Bruce's brain damage was described, and Dr. Smith said it was difficult to treat. Drugs, and, perhaps, surgical therapy, could be effective, he said.

Under cross-examination by Crown prosecutor Andrejz Berzins, Dr. Smith stood by his conclusions, and testified Bruce belonged in a psychiatric institution.

"Couldn't a penitentiary offer Mr. Hamill adequate care?" Berzins asked.

"That's a pious hope," Dr. Smith answered.

Other psychiatrist testified that Hamill didn't understand the nature and consequences of his crime.

Although Hamill knew killing Wentzlaff was wrong, "he didn't feel it was wrong," said Dr. Frank Chalke, a consulting psychiatrist at the Royal Ottawa Hospital.

"Originally, I felt that he did know. He planned on doing it. He formed the intention to do it.

"But during the summer, I received the medical evidence that showed Mr. Hamill has a brain disorder that affects his ability to think. I had to change my diagnosis," he said.

Dr. Elliott Barker was called to testify for the prosecution. Dr. Barker no longer believed that psychopaths belonged in the hospital system. He told the jury that Hamill acted logically, that everything the killer did was based on his loyalty to his family and his lack of concern for Betty Wentzlaff.

"During my interview with him, Mr. Hamill showed a frightening lack of empathy. He told me 'I felt like I was going to the corner store and buying a bag of chips when I stabbed her'.

"This boy is disturbed in a number of ways, none of which fit him for the criminal code definition of insanity," Dr. Barker added. Dr. Russell Fleming also testified for the prosecution, although he was careful to explain that Hamill's brain disorder could have been the cause of his violent outbursts. He told the jury about Hamill's lack of regret for the killing, how he worried about being sent to prison. The crime, Dr. Fleming explained, had meant almost nothing to Hamill. Still, there were signs that the young man didn't like living with his rages, and showed some real determination to be rid of them.

Dr. David Bulmer, a psychiatrist at the Royal Ottawa Hospital, testified that Hamill's strange behaviour at the time of the murder was evidence that he was having an epileptic fit brought on by his brain damage.

The night before the killing, Hamill took a "sick pathological step in thinking that the something that had to be done was that she should be shot down. It would not have occurred to him that there were other ways of dealing with the situation."

Yes, Dr. Bulmer admitted under cross examination by prosecutor Berzins, Hamill was aware that he was stabbing Mrs. Wentzlaff and that she was going to die, "but at the time, he did not know that what he was doing was wrong."

Afterwards, he realized the wrongness of his actions, but felt they "were not part of himself. Something had happened to him he felt was beyond his control. While he's undergoing a discharge, Bruce doesn't have the ability to make any meaningful choices."

Berzins fought the insanity defence, accusing Dr. Bulmer of trying to absolve Hamill of his responsibility for Wentzlaff's death by blaming his diseased mind, but Dr. Bulmer argued forcefully that Hamill really did lose touch with reality when he had his fits.

The day after Dr. Bulmer testified, the eleven men and one woman on the jury retired for two hours before delivering their verdict that they found Hamill not guilty by reason of insanity.

He stayed at Oak Ridge from January 1978 until December, 1980, then was transferred to Brockville. At that institution, he was given day passes and gradually prepared for release. In March, 1983, Hamill was freed. Five years later, he was discharged from his Warrant of the Lieutenant-Governor, the court order issued after the insanity verdict.

Nine years after killing Betty Wentzlaff, Hamill had no criminal record. He would, according to institutional policy, make a fit escort for Krueger on his first citizen-supervised day pass.

THE C-4 RITUAL

Who was I before I was me?
How many times have I lived?
Why so many I can't see?
When will I set my mind free?

Guided by an invisible force
So close but unknown to me

Not out a reach, just going thru a course
In time I'll find who I seek.

If it was me who I see
I wouldn't be so surprised
As sooner or later I'll realize
it's just me, finding my way!

-Dennis Kerr, 1989

The Brockville Psychiatric Hospital is a peaceful place, set in a small town on the banks of the St. Lawrence River, about an hour's drive south of Ottawa. Brockville is quite similar to Penetanguishene: it's having tough economic times. The hospital, which, in 1997, was ordered by the Harris government to close, was one of the main employers. Brockville Psychiatric Hospital provided its staff with good pay in return for looking after some of the nastiest people in Canada. Usually, people there tried to forget about the hospital, especially the forty dangerous inmates of its forensic unit. For years, Brockville was the destination of choice for Penetanguishene's serial killers. Far from the glare of the media, they were able to get freedoms that would be, in Toronto, blocked by publicity. Clinical staff at Brockville had the reputation of being free and easy with day passes, and the hospital ran a first-rate recreational program: they even took Krueger to see *The Silence of the Lambs*.

"I sided with Hannibal Lector," he told me, years later, when he was back in Oak Ridge. "I could relate to how badly they treated him."

Even more thrilling, they drove Krueger to the railway museum in the nearby town of Smith Falls. Brockville is on the main line of the railway that links Toronto and Montreal. Krueger liked to watch the trains go by from his hospital window. Dennis Kerr, who would sit in the woods near the track and play his flute, liked the trains, too.

For about eighteen months, Brockville prepared Krueger for life in the outside world. There, he was made to feel as though there was life after all of those years locked up in

Penetanguishene. Staff took him on two trips to Montreal, a couple of short sight-seeing trips in Ottawa, and to a university night school class. They worked on getting Krueger help from the Canadian National Institute for the Blind. They made it clear that Brockville would support a transfer to a low-security rehabilitation ward in Ontario, or even in another province where no one remembered Peter Woodcock. That's why the exercise failed: Krueger didn't really want to get out. He began to spin his fantasy webs in the Brockville institution.

The treatment team of a psychiatrist, a psychologist, nurses, occupational and recreational therapists worked hard to get Krueger released. They seemed to like him. If they hadn't been so eager to help Krueger leave, they might have heard the hints that trouble was coming. Gaetan Chartrand, a patient on Krueger's ward, told staff that Krueger had suggested they run away together and "kill some kids". Krueger denied the allegation and staff let the matter drop. Chartrand was telling the truth. The Brotherhood, or something like it, was taking shape again. All Krueger needed were some warm bodies to act as eyes, ears and hands for him.

The first man he caught in this Brotherhood web was Hamill. Krueger offered him help for his brain damage, the reincarnation of his father, who had died during the years Hamill had been locked up, and a seat on a spaceship that was supposed to leave for the home planet of The Brotherhood in 2011. Hamill offered Krueger companionship, sex and, because he had been freed, a link to the outside world. In early 1991, Hamill started his train trips to Brockville.

"He was called Battling Bruce on the busses of Ottawa because he used to beat up drivers and passengers," Krueger says. "Bruce really got shafted. His condition was diagnosed at the Royal Ottawa, but that diagnosis wasn't recognized here. He has some sort of systemic malfunction. There is a place where Bruce could go to, where he could get that cleared up. It's in the States, in Vermont. There's also a place in the States where they can treat teenage disorders. If I had gone there, I would be out today and a lot of cops would be out of work."

Against the advice of some of their staff, officials of the

Brockville hospital signed the papers that approved Hamill as a supervisor for Krueger's trips off the hospital grounds. A new policy allowed dangerous patients to be escorted into the community by "sponsors". Only convicted criminals and people tagged with Lieutenant-Governor's warrants were ineligible to be sponsors. Krueger was among the first patients admitted to the citizen escort program.

Hamill was eligible as a sponsor because, in the eyes of the law, he had never been a risk to anyone. A hospital spokesperson later said Hamill had been given careful scrutiny, but she added that, because of his lack of a criminal record, "you have to treat him the way you would treat anyone else, and ignore, I guess, these things in his background."

On 13 July 1991, Hamill, a good-looking, muscular man who, like so many Oak Ridge alumni, looks younger than his age, told his wife he was going on a camping trip. Instead, he took the train from Ottawa to Brockville to help kill Dennis Kerr.

These days, Krueger says he's dropped out of the Guards. Looking back to the time of the murder, he says the stress of his imminent release after so many years locked up caused his fantasy life to go wild. It had sustained him in his empty youth and had come roaring back when the responsibilities of freedom appeared to be getting closer.

"It sounds kind of stupid, but Bruce believed it because he would do anything to get rid of his problems. I simply gave him an opportunity, and he took it. I was under a lot of stress at the time, and I was really believing in this stuff, too," Krueger said.

Kerr was no angel, nor a stranger to violence. He had stabbed and wounded a woman in Welland during a break-in when he was nineteen-years-old. Kerr was in the woman's house, looking for money for drugs, when the elderly woman walked in. He had spent more than half of his life in some kind of custody.

Kerr considered himself a maverick and was a constant critic of Oak Ridge. He was a good source of information for the reporters who covered mental health care issues. His attacks on the system were used by Krueger to justify the killing. Kerr was being processed for release from Brockville, but Krueger claims the psychiatric system really wasn't going to let Kerr go.

"If I had believed they were seriously thinking about letting Kerr go, I would have picked someone else," Krueger says. "Now he's out of the hands of the review board. He's in a better place."

Kerr might have argued that he was in a good enough place in Brockville.

* * *

Looking back on the Kerr killing, Krueger sees it as a botched crime.

"Had it been left up to me, it would have happened with no one knowing about it, it would have been done in such a way that no one could link me to it. Bruce was about as subtle as Lord Cardigan at the Charge of the Light Brigade. I was surprised that it was going down, but once it started, there was no going back. I became afraid that, if Dennis woke up to what happened, I could get hurt. He was a very violent person. I gave Bruce the spark and he ran with it. If Bruce had said no, it never would have happened. I did instigate it, and he helped implement it."

"It's very uncharacteristic for me to cry, but I cried for two weeks after that. There were so many different reasons to cry. Certainly, I cried because of what had happened to Dennis, because he certainly didn't ask us to do that. I cried for me, I cried for Bruce. I couldn't bring myself to face anybody, and I told the guards when I went in that 'I don't want no phone calls, no visits, no messages in or out'. If they had just taken me straight to the penitentiary, put me in a cell or dungeon and just closed the door, I could have stayed there for eternity. It would have been just.

"I slept through most of that Sunday. That afternoon, they took me upstairs to administrative segregation, the hole. I looked at other people, they looked at me. The younger people were friendly. I slept on the floor that night, but the next day, they made arrangements for me, and I was put in a cell that I would stay in for the rest of the time that I was in Brockville. My upper bunkmate was involved in the Prescott sex scandal."

Hamill was kept in the main jail population, but Krueger was held in protective custody. Within a few days, Krueger realized that, barring a freak of justice that would send him to a federal prison, he was likely heading back to Oak Ridge. Meanwhile, he tried to keep out of trouble.

"I was afraid of being admitted to the main population. In the days that followed, I was really scared. They took me down to the provincial courthouse for my first arraignment on a Monday, two days afterwards. There were some reporters around. There weren't too many, though.

"I kind of liked the Brockville jail. It was small and the guards did their duty, you know. It was noisy, on occasion, but not bad. You could go down and see the young offenders in their red T-shirts. Some of the 'youngsters' looked more vicious than a lot of the regular inmates."

The Brockville jail also shielded Krueger from the backlash to the murder, as long as he stayed away from the radio, TV and newspapers. The Toronto media, especially the *Sun*, had jumped on the case as an example of what happens when dangerous people like Krueger are given freedom. The paper was fuzzy on the details of Kerr's murder, but columnist Christie Blatchford, a long-time critic of Oak Ridge and the forensic psychiatry system, summed up many readers' views when she wrote, "until we learn what to do with the Woodcock-Kruegers our society seems so good at producing, why do we persist in believing they will get better and putting other people at risk?"

By the time they went to bed, the 400 patients in the Brockville Psychiatric Hospital had heard of Kerr's death. They had been gathered together in groups and told of the killing. Kerr was mourned by the forensic unit patients, who took to the phones to tell their contacts in the media that they knew a killing like this was bound to happen. One inmate, rapist Daryl Jones, told a *Toronto Star* reporter that he had complained to Brockville Psychiatric Hospital staff about the day pass system.

Three years later, Jones was released to a Brockville halfway house. A few weeks later, he murdered an elderly woman. He's now serving a seventeen-year penitentiary sentence for second degree murder.

* * *

From that Saturday night until their trial eighteen months later, Krueger and Hamill were moved from jail to jail in eastern Ontario. Krueger hated the boredom of solitary confinement, where he was kept to protect him from prisoners who would have killed him for being the lowest form of jail life, a molester and a "goof". For a while, he had a cellmate, a minister who was charged in a child sex ring, but most of the time, he just had walls to look at. Krueger missed his short wave set. Guards gave him a small transistor radio that he used to pick up local AM stations. It was a mere shadow of those powerful radios that could pull in signals from Europe, Africa, and the stations in Appalachia where strange men whisper into microphones about Armageddon. By late fall of 1992, Krueger and Hamill finally had something to do to kill time. Lawyers came and went. Hearings were held to set a trial date and to change the trial venue from Brockville to Ottawa. Psychiatrists, including Krueger's old friend John Atcheson, who he had known since his arrest in 1957, came to examine him. Finally, the trial began in the bunker-like Ottawa-Carleton regional courthouse a few blocks from the Parliament Buildings. The capital was lit for Christmas, and as the paddy wagon that brought Krueger from the local jail cruised along the city's main expressway and across the Rideau Canal, the killer could see the neo-Gothic towers of the old legislative buildings glowing with thousands of tiny lightbulbs. As he rode, locked away in a special isolation compartment with one tiny window, other prisoners thumped on the wall and hollered about the "diddler" inside. Krueger easily ignored them.

People on the downtown streets shivered against the cold as they went to work, but Krueger was snug in his little compartment. Prisoners are brought to the courthouse's lockups from an underground parking lot, which helps thwart news photographers and television camera operators. Krueger was grateful for the heat and privacy. He waited in his little steel closet until the other prisoners were led off, then he was taken out, his leg irons and handcuff chains rattling in the concrete loading area.

The trial began 9 December, 1992, and was expected to be over by Christmas. The court quickly got down to business. Hamill, looking rather dazed, pleaded not guilty first, then Krueger rose, straightened himself, and said, "not guilty, my lord", when called on by the court clerk. He always liked saying "my lord". He remembered doing it at his first trial, and had fantasized about it for years. Rarely did he have the attention of someone as important as an Ontario Supreme Court judge. Krueger hoped the judge liked him.

Detective Bishop, who had tackled Hamill at the murder scene, was one of the first witnesses to testify. He was asked about Krueger's name change. Bishop still wasn't sure whether it was connected to Freddie Krueger of Elm Street fame. He had another theory: that the new name honoured a Nazi general who had supposedly recruited people for death squads. Both ideas were wrong. The name change happened before the horror movie came out. And there was no Nazi general with that name; in fact, the opposite was the case. During World War II, U.S. General Walter Krueger commanded soldiers during the Allied invasion of the Philippines. The reason didn't matter, anyway, Bishop theorized. The name change wasn't done to pay tribute to anyone. That would be an act of generosity beyond Krueger's psychopathic limitations. Like everything else Krueger did, the name change was an act of selfishness.

"He felt if he changed his name from Peter Woodcock, he would get rid of the alien beings in his body and it would be a fresh start," Bishop testified. That, and the fact that Krueger was more aggressive-sounding and less open to nasty puns, was the reason for the name change.

Bishop had never seen Krueger when he wasn't soaring on his fantasies. He believed Krueger was unable to step back from his alien dreamland. Bishop didn't realize that Krueger could bury his fantasies deep enough to maintain semi-normal relationships with sane people. Then he could use them when he met someone weak enough to con. When he was alone, the fantasies acted like an illicit drug.

Seeing Krueger soaring on his evil at the time of the Hamill murder, Bishop got a look at the onion-like layers of Krueger's psyche. He saw how he had taken naive, damaged Hamill and used him as a weapon. Bishop summed Krueger in two words: "con man". Then he told the silent courtroom how Krueger was so sexually aroused the slaughter of Kerr that he spent the night of the murder masturbating in his cell.

Bishop took the spectators in the courtroom on a step-by-step verbal tour of the murder, explained how Hamill had been duped into believing that he would soon be in New York, courtesy of the Guard. He described, to Hamill's surprise and horror, how Krueger had stroked his co-accused's breastbone with the hunting knife, pondering whether to bury the blade in his heart, because Hamill had botched the C-4 ritual by killing Kerr before he sodomized him.

Bishop's testimony established Krueger and Hamill's guilt. The next day, Dr. Atcheson's testimony saved Krueger from prison again. Dr. Atcheson's testimony would send Hamill back to Oak Ridge, too.

Dr. Atcheson testified that Krueger was still enjoying the murder of Kerr when he visited the killer in the Brockville jail a month earlier. When he described Kerr's death, Krueger had broken down and cried, not because he felt bad for what he did or afraid of what his punishment would be, but "because Kerr had died such a noble death. He was deeply moved and hoped his death would be as noble."

Dr. Atcheson described Krueger's ability to "sell the delusion" of the Guards, how his skills as a con man had been honed during his thirty-four years locked up in Oak Ridge and the other institutions. He told how the fantasies had been born in the mind of a twisted, lonely child as "The Winchester Heights Gang", how, after years of drug therapy and social skills training, they had become more complex, more sinister, as "The Brotherhood", "The Family", "The Inter-Galactic Police" and "The Praetorian Guard". Krueger had told Dr. Atcheson that the years of therapy had cured him.

"I believe he thought it was true," Atcheson testified. "I didn't think it was true. The delusion is always there. At the time of the killings, he was completely in this alien world."

Krueger looked down at his hands. A newspaper reporter in the courtroom caught his eye. The reporter jotted into his notebook: "short, dumpy, with thinning hair".

When Krueger read the *Ottawa Citizen* the next day, he thought it was bad enough that his private life was spread out for everyone to see, without being insulted about the way he looked. He was also disappointed that the story of his trial was buried in the back of the paper.

Usually, it takes the unchallenged testimony of two psychiatrists to convince a Canadian court that an accused person is insane. In this trial, three were called, each taking a day at the end of the week-long trial. Forensic psychiatrist Graham Terrall told the court that it was clear to him that Krueger's madness was untreatable. Krueger sat stone-faced as Dr. Terrall testified about Krueger's masturbation sessions in the hours after the killing, how he couldn't keep his hands off himself in the Brockville hospital or the police lockup.

For Krueger, killing someone was "like smashing a doll," Dr. Terrall said.

The following Monday, Selwyn Smith, the psychiatrist who examined Hamill, testified how the dupe had believed Krueger's promise of life-long help from the Guards, how Hamill was conned into thinking he was in line for a big government security job or re-settlement in the Philippines, how, killing Kerr would be, as Dr. Smith testified, "a good career move."

Crown attorney John Vamplew, who could have fought the insanity defence and argued that Krueger and Hamill should be jailed for life, did not debate with the psychiatrist. He described Krueger and Hamill as "one sickness feeding the other." Dr. Smith agreed.

"In my view," Dr. Smith answered, "this is mental illness personified. He (Hamill) was not making this up. He honestly believed in the sequence of things as though they were real. He still believes the Guard will look after him," Dr. Smith said.

"He must, without any shadow of a doubt, be regarded as dangerous."

The next afternoon, Justice Douglas Rutherford found the two killers not criminally responsible for Kerr's murder because of their mental disorders.

Judge Rutherford described the fantasy that snared Hamill: "Krueger's earlier delusions ... had apparently evolved into an elaborate setting in which there existed an Imperial Order of the Guard, understandable only with the benefit of Krueger's understanding of history, philosophy and religion.

"This Guard, or Praetorian Guard, as he sometimes referred to it, was a powerful and resource-filled organization, the membership of which included many prominent, rich and powerful persons. The Guard was connected to a galactic law enforcement power and its actions and objectives were in consonance with Divine Will.

"Krueger was a field service representative of the Guard and recruited members. He had convinced a number of inmates over the years to believe in and join his delusional organization. Entry to the Guard and access to its help and resources was subject to initiation rites, as was promotion to various levels within it. These rites of passage involved homosexual and sadistic acts," the judge said.

"This was very real to them."

A few days later, both killers were back at Oak Ridge. Hamill finally began to realize that Krueger had lied. The guard hadn't saved him at the murder scene. They hadn't broken him out of jail or come for him at the trial. He was back in the grim green halls of Oak Ridge, with years to ponder what had happened.

Krueger was back, too, in another part of the institution. He saw lots of familiar faces, they still made that wonderful fried chicken every two weeks, and, with luck, the box with his shortwave sets would arrive from Brockville soon.

The police were disappointed with the outcome of Krueger's trial. They wanted to see Krueger end up in prison. After his months in jail, waiting for trial, Krueger said prison didn't seem like such a bad fate.

"They kept me in protective custody but at least they didn't pretend I was in some kind of hospital. When I went to court, they would put me on a bus that stopped at the other jails in eastern Ontario.

"I got to meet a lot of people and see a lot of that part of Ontario that way. When the bus passed a shapely girl, all of the heads would snap in her direction. It was a lot of fun," he said.

* * *

Kerr's family sued the health ministry and the hospitals involved in the release of Krueger and Hamill, eventually settling for an undisclosed amount of money.

Muriel Soleby, Kerr's mother, said her son hadn't deserved to die: "He was down by the railway tracks writing music (when Hamill and Krueger asked him to go into the woods). To this day, I don't know what happened. All I know is I got my son back in a black box. I couldn't look at him. I had him cremated in Toronto."

As for Dennis, well, that was all his fault, Krueger says. Or it was the fault of the Review Board. Or it was the fault of Kerr's family.

"The family of Dennis, if they had listened to him, they would not have had to bring the lawsuit. I very deeply regret that what happened, happened. I do take some comfort from it. At least, as far as he is concerned, he's beyond reach of the review board. They screwed him something wicked. This is the problem: if you go to prison, you get so much time, and then you get out. Part of the problem, at my trial, the Crown says that (raising his voice, becoming preachy) 'he was on his way out of the system. The prognosis was excellent'. I thought to myself 'they didn't tell him that'. If they had told him that, he would probably still be alive.

"If he had any kind of a future, I wouldn't have killed him. Really, he is beyond all pain and suffering and anxiety. This whole thing is really comforting. If anything good can be taken from this, it's that he's no longer under the thumb of the review board."

* * *

The community reaction was predictable and understandable. Within a few weeks of the murder, 5,000 residents of the Brockville area signed a petition calling for tighter controls on the release of potentially dangerous patients.

People in Brockville wanted to know how murderers could be allowed to wander the grounds of the hospital, and how Hamill, a killer, could have been approved as Krueger's escort. Management of the hospital told the press that they were following hospital policy. When I asked hospital public relations director Nora White in 1994, three years after the killing, if she saw any reason to amend those policies, she said no.

Brockville citizens used picket signs and demonstrations to draw attention to the lack of concern for public safety. A committee of hospital officials and town councillors was set up to try to diffuse the situation, but the meetings turned out to be something of a waste of time. Mayor Stephen Clark and Leeds-Grenville MPP Bob Runciman, became involved. The Brockville hospital's escort policy "just boggles the mind," Runciman was quoted as saying. As an opposition MPP, he had no power, but in 1994, he became Ontario's Solicitor General, and nothing changed.

Blame was passed from hand to hand: hospital administrators said the review board sets the level of patient freedom. The review board said Parliament had drafted their mandate. No one accepted responsibility for what happened to Kerr. Since nothing changed, another killing could happen just as easily, and, as it turned out, it did, when Daryl Jones was released.

Jones had been found not guilty by reason of insanity of the attempted murder, rape and robbery of a Toronto woman in 1975. The former busboy had used the media to help him get out of Oak Ridge, carefully crafting himself as a victim of a heartless system who was being unjustly treated. He had invited sympathetic reporters to his review board hearings in the days when they were closed to the public. In Brockville, he had kept the press informed of the inmate backlash to the Krueger killing.

On Boxing Day, 1993, police arrested Jones and charged him with the September killing of a seventy-nine-year-old widow. In the wake of the Kerr murder, officials of the Attorney General's ministry had tried to fight Jones' release, proving that he had violated the terms of his Lieutenant Governor's warrant several times. The review board let him out anyway.

The Attorney General's office went to court to challenge the board's ruling, but by the time the Ontario Court of Appeal came down with a decision ordering Jones to be locked up again, it was too late. The Court slammed the review board system and the hospital staff, saying their decisions were "unreasonable" and a "complete abdication of responsibility". They noted that Jones had resisted treatment and showed no improvement while in Brockville.

"One is driven reluctantly to the conclusion that the review board simply caved in to the pressure from hospital staff to relieve them of the responsibility of supervising [Jones]."

In 1994, a tough new chief psychiatrist was transferred to Brockville by the NDP government. Neil Conacher, who had been the head of psychiatry at Kingston Penitentiary, was expected to straighten out the institution's many problems. Cons in Kingston knew him for his aggressive use of the Mental Health Act to lock up prison inmates who had served their time but who, in Dr. Conacher's view, were too dangerous to let out. Time passed uneventfully at Brockville until the hospital was closed by the province's health care restructuring committee. Now there are even fewer psychiatric hospital beds in Ontario.

These days, Hamill now lives on the same Ward 04 of Oak Ridge, a high-privilege unit that is home to most of Canada's worst serial killers. He's expected to be released or sent to a medium security hospital within the next few years.

KRUEGER'S WORLD

I met Krueger about a year after the Kerr murder, but it wasn't a crime that I had spent much time thinking about. It, along with Frederick's murder of Christopher Stephenson, Gillis and Abel's attack in London, and several other Oak Ridge inmate crimes seemed to be just so much background noise. Krueger was enjoying the notoriety of being a serial killer at a time when movies like *The Silence of the Lambs* made complex murderers seem glamorous. At the same time, Krueger was gloomy that his life had become so predictable, that he faced another twenty or thirty years in Oak Ridge, then death and a funeral with no mourners. He knew the hype about serial killers was pure Hollywood. Serial killers came and went from the Oak Ridge canteen as we talked, buying bags of chips and packs of cigarettes. They looked like guys grabbed at random from a bar, big, pasty-faced, pot-bellied men wearing bad clothes.

"I don't see serial killers as really being that separate from everybody else," Krueger said to me one day. "There may be a need by society to think that such people are different, not like us at all. But the sad reality is that they aren't. I think we can't answer the broader question of 'why do some children end up having criminal minds and are much more interested in criminal behaviour than other kids? Some kids do drugs, and others don't. All kinds of criminality is different. Some kids who are criminals don't smoke pot or crack or mainline horse (heroin) or whatever. Around here, you listen to people talk about themselves and the encounters they have had in their lives, then you listen to a so-called normal person talk about their life experiences, and, if there is any common factor, it seems to be that those who have transgressed are weaker in their moral makeup, and they basically don't have a code of ethics. It's all for me. Everything I do is OK. It's an ultimate selfishness. Many people who are mentally ill are totally self-centred," he said.

It was a very astute personal assessment, and one that is rarely worked into therapy. Krueger saw his need to rape and kill as a character flaw, an act of utter selfishness. Nowhere in his huge clinical file was that idea ever addressed, yet it made perfect sense. The fantasy world was a place owned an operated by Krueger, a place where he could do anything he wanted. Outside of it, he began to never say no to himself.

"There's a big different between the neurotic housewife and the psychopath," Krueger went on to say. "Even if a serial killer thinks the world is there for his pleasure, so what? Does that make him crazy? Pol Pot, the dictator of the Khmer Rouge in Kampuchea, killed a million people in genocide. The American calvary that committed genocide against the North American aboriginals, they were engaged in a war of genocide. There isn't any difference between those people and a narcissistic killer like me or Russ Johnson (who was in Oak Ridge for killing between seven and fifteen women).

"I don't see any difference between myself and my foster father, who soldiered in the First World War and who killed many of the enemy. He probably killed more people than me. But he was in a uniform, people blew trumpets and played drums, and cheering crowds turned out to see him off to head out to kill other young men. But because somebody like me committed the atrocities, and they were atrocities, let's face it, that were offensive to anybody who had the right mindset, I suppose, but then, ask a father about somebody like me who has raped his daughter, and he'll want to string up somebody like me and have every conceivably painful thing done to me. But we hear names like Sarajevo and Mostar, and there are grown men killing children there. It's politics."

The difference, in politics, and, I'll admit, it's a weak one, is that there is some purpose to organized killing. And, on just as shaky ground, I would argue that the difference between a soldier in World War I and Krueger is the soldier's ability to feel some of the pain of his victim, and to say no to himself if he had the urge to kill after the war was over. I suspect the way people were raised in the Middle Ages helped them develop into the psychopaths who thrived in the never-ending cycle of warfare. Any good biography of the rulers of England shows that there wasn't a lot of bonding going on between mothers and babies in the royal family, and, even today, it's grossly dysfunctional. John Keegan, the brilliant British journalist who used to teach at the Sandhurst military academy, argues that most killing in battle is done when one side tries to run. Medieval battles were scenes of incredible slaughter. Battles such as Stirling Bridge, recreated in the movie Braveheart, were scenes of butchery, rather than slaughter. The lyrical public image of two knights fighting should, perhaps, be replaced with one ragged peasant stabbing another one in the back.

Modern writers argue that the Nazis turned a whole country into psychopaths, or at least tapped into a murderous streak in the German people that, according to William Shirer, runs through their history. I doubt that. Any society produces more than enough psychopaths to staff gas chambers, shoot hostages and run slave labour factories. In societies that don't condone their excesses, they find other things to run or take up space in the jails. Psychopaths walk a tightrope, not having the ethical core to make decisions for themselves, relying on the reaction of society to show them how to behave. Society rejected Krueger, and he killed. Society rejected Hitler, and he went into politics.

"In each of us there are flaws that allow us to do the bad things we do, and there are strengths that prevent us from doing even worse things," Krueger said one day. "I wonder if that strength just never develops in some of us. I heard about a case recently of a baby born in Newfoundland without eyes. People are born with terrible physical deformities. With all the panoply of physical deformities and diseases, the mental deficiencies we can't see are a whole other gamut. You see children with terrible deformities, Siamese twins and babies born with their hands sticking out of the shoulders, and no one puts any blame on them. Yet they put the blame on me," Krueger says.

On 22 April, 1993, Krueger sat fuming in the office of his social worker. Less than two years had passed since he and Hamill had butchered Dennis Kerr. The review board had recently heard his request for an out-of-province transfer, and had turned him down. The social worker read the disposition order, Krueger slammed his hand down on the man's desk and stormed out, hollering that he would call his lawyer.

A few seconds later, Krueger was back in the office, composed, talking reasonably about his fear that friends of Dennis Kerr would try to kill him. Kerr had been part of the harems of several of the more dangerous inmates on Ward 04, the wing where most of the long-term psychopathic patients are held. And Hamill was still after him, too, Krueger insisted. He apologized for his angry outburst. He began to relax. He talked about his sex drive, how he had once been a pedophile but now was only interested in young males, especially those of slim build, with little body hair. He went on to say that, if he could have sex with a woman and enjoy that, this might cure his homosexuality.

Six months later, the inquest into Kerr's death finally began in Brockville. Krueger had nagged me for more than a year to go to Brockville and sit through it. Somehow, he thought, the hearing would vindicate him, or, at least, put more of the blame for the Kerr killing onto Hamill. Inquests in Ontario can't assign criminal responsibility, only the courts can do that, but they often end with recommendations that make it clear where members of the jury feel blame should go. The inquest did nothing to help Krueger's reputation. Too many people had an interest in putting all the blame on him.

The Kerr inquest was infested with lawyers who would spend months haggling over the amount of information from the killers' clinical records that the jury could see. Krueger told me he wanted to testify, but that was blocked, too. More than eighty witnesses gave evidence, but most of the incriminating information in Krueger's file was kept from the jury. Lawyers representing the health ministry, the Brockville hospital and the review board supported Krueger's lawyer's arguments to keep the file closed, for their own reasons. A three-member panel of Divisional Court decided to allow limited access to Krueger and Hamill's clinical records, but all the jury really needed to hear was the testimony of Oak Ridge chief psychiatrist Russel Fleming and Dr. Stephen Hucker, head of the Clarke Institute of Psychiatry's forensic service, who had assessed Krueger before the review board sent him to Brockville.

Dr. Hucker told the inquest how he had opposed Krueger's transfer to Brockville from Oak Ridge, that Krueger was, in his view, still an obsessed sexual sadist and psychopath who couldn't be re-integrated into the community.

Oak Ridge chief psychiatrist Russel Fleming agreed with people who live in North Bay, St. Thomas and Brockville, the homes of the medium security institutions where many of Oak Ridge's inmates are sent to, that the provincial government was loading the dice against citizens of those communities.

"No matter how careful you are, there will be failures," he said, "but if you have a unit that brings into your community a large number of risky people, you are likely to raise the risk for the local population. The reality is that clinical judgements of psychiatrists, in terms of assessing risk, was about as effective as flipping a coin. It was notoriously unreliable. That's why we have serious problems."

It wasn't a quote that would be inscribed on any monuments, but it made the people of Brockville feel that someone in the system realized that their community was carrying a heavier burden than other towns. Dr. Fleming modestly didn't mention the warning he made against Krueger's transfer to Brockville, or the fact that he told staff at Brockville that the serial killer couldn't even be trusted on the hospital's grounds. In his frank testimony at the inquest, Dr. Fleming painted a devastating picture of a system that hurries violent inmates along because of a shortage of beds and money. He said the system can save money by moving some more trustworthy patients from the prison-like conditions of Oak Ridge to less secure institutions, but he criticized the policy of letting psychopathic killers out onto the street.

"I don't care much if people move out of maximum security into medium, even if they are potentially dangerous. But I am not keen to have them move to medium security if the end result is they will move into that community where citizens will be at risk," he testified.

In other words, Krueger could have had the comfort of life at Brockville, with its staff-escorted day trips and its rehabilitation programs, as long as he wasn't given the chance to be on his own or allowed out with other killers. It seems like a simple solution, but with hospital cutbacks, there would always be someone waiting for Krueger's hospital bed and cost-cutters demanding to know why so many people were being held for so long. Since governments are cutting budgets for places like Oak Ridge and closing hospitals like Brockville, the chances of more Kruegers being hurried through the system has only increased since the Kerr murder. In 1993, under the NDP's "Putting People First" program, a sweet name for more cutbacks, the province began a program to slash psychiatric hospital beds from 58 per 100,000 to about half that. Provincial bureaucrats know that de-institutionalization hasn't worked. In its preamble to the "Putting People First" report, the health ministry said "Because services are not well co-ordinated, (patients) may be shuffled from one place to another, assessed again and again and still not receive appropriate services."

Since then, there has been a steady decline in the amount of money given to the system, and no real reform to deal with the cutbacks. For public safety's sake, there must be a whole new treatment and incarceration system designed for violent psychopaths, whether they are in jail or mental institutions.

In the United States, which is farther down the road to de-institutionalization, critics claim more than 100,000 de-institutionalized former psychiatric patients are homeless and another 30,000 are in jail. A 1989 Canadian survey said 15 per cent of provincial jail inmates have serious mental problems. The figure is higher for federal prisoners. On the streets, social workers have case loads of 300 or more. Many mentally ill people steal just so they will be caught and taken off the streets.

In Canada, the bigger cities, with beggars on every block, are home to thousands of untreated mentally ill people. Parkdale in Toronto, Portage and Main in Winnipeg, Ottawa's Elgin Street and Lowertown, and Montreal's Atwater district have become the haunts of the mentally ill homeless. Eventually, the cost will have to be paid, whether it's in welfare payments, chronic care for diseases such as tuberculosis, which is roaring back among street people, or on care for people with disorders caused by malnourishment. Or worse, the cost will be carried by the families of victims of violently mentally ill people who have been released too soon, or who should never have been let out. An Oak Ridge study of 467 violent mental patients who had been in the system since 1990 found that one in six offenders would likely commit another violent act within seven years. Half of the people surveyed were already on the street in 1993. Police officials like London chief Julian Fantino joined psychiatrists in demanding better care for people after they were let out of hospitals. Essentially, someone has to stay close to former patients to make sure they keep taking their medications, and be able to yank them back into the hospital if they show signs of deterioration.

People can't have it both ways: if there are going to be tax cuts and balanced budgets, the money must come from somewhere. The same people who advocate locking dangerous people up for life also want smaller government. More simplistic people call for a return of capital punishment, but the defence of insanity will always be there, and Canada will never execute the insane. The last country to do that was Nazi Germany, although the U.S., with its recent executions of mentally disabled killers, is beginning to cross the line.

Still, there's no excuse for the kind of stupidity that haunted the management of the Brockville hospital. Even without the major changes that the system needs, there is still no reason why exquisitely dangerous people like Krueger should be allowed to be escorted out of an institution by other killers. What made the Brockville case so infuriating to those who followed it, especially the people of the community, was the refusal of the institution to accept any responsibility for it. The former administrator, Patrick Lee, testified at the inquest that he saw no reason to make any changes at the Brockville hospital because: "The guidelines were followed, the policies were followed." His former boss, Howard Danson, the director of the Ministry of Health's mental facilities branch, backed him up: "The policies and procedures in place were followed."

It didn't seem to matter to them that the policies and procedures were rotten in the first place. These policies and procedures, which are created without real public input, have been licenses to kill for Fredericks, Krueger, and many other ex-Oak Ridge inmates.

Daryl Jones' arrest for the murder of Ruth Cohen came a few weeks after Dr. Fleming's testimony and at the half-way point of the Kerr inquest. By then, the people of Brockville were livid, but the local council tried to dampen the anger so that the 800 jobs provided by the Brockville hospital wouldn't be threatened.

The inquest jury made more than 100 recommendations. It wanted police to be notified when a potentially dangerous patient is released; a national central registry for known sex offenders, and a national treatment centre for them; reasonable public access to Criminal Code Review Board hearings; and tougher laws dealing with sexual predators.

The less costly recommendations have been followed. The review board has opened up its hearings to the public and publishes its decisions. New, tougher dangerous offender laws have been brought in by the federal government. Still, the system that deals with psychopaths like Krueger hasn't changed much.

People like Elliott Barker argue much of the money spent on treating psychopaths could be saved by strengthening families. He's on solid ground. All of the files I've read on Canadian serial killers show that they had nightmare childhoods, usually bounced around as babies from one foster home to another. Krueger's childhood is absolutely typical of his fellow psychopathic murderers. He believes that genetic programming makes the difference, but that babies in the womb know whether they are wanted. "I often wonder what happened in my own pre-birth, whether my natural mother wanted me. I'm glad I wasn't aborted. If someone commits abortion, they should be executed. Let the babies be brought to term and put up for adoption. Of course, if you read about the first three years of my life, before I was adopted, it would curl your hair and straighten it back out again."

One day, while we talked in the Oak Ridge visitor centre, a woman was working, setting a table with a lace tablecloth, picnic basket, and a vase full of purple flowers. A huge patient, nearly seven feet tall, joined her for the romantic lunch. Soft Phil Collins music played over the loudspeakers.

Krueger peered at the couple, and began feeling lonely.

"There aren't as many visits as there used to be. If it wasn't for you, I wouldn't get any at all," Krueger said. "People are in here for such a long time, and for the people out there, time doesn't stop. People keep growing and moving forward. Everyone I knew before I came here has died or given up on me. Being alone in the world has been both a blessing and a curse for me. The fact there is nobody out there waiting for me makes me rest more easy. If there had been someone waiting for me all of these years, I would be bitter."

I asked him what life would be like if someone invented a quick cure for his psychopathy and the Oak Ridge doors swung open to let him go. Krueger said he would work for a while, until he had some money, and would settle in Russia. He says Russia's history is like his own. The country has been in bondage for so many years. So, in his own mind, has Krueger. The short wave radio has been Krueger's real link to the world, his little electronic friend that, quite often, brings him samples of the rest of the world's insanity. After the Kerr killing, Oak Ridge staff tried to punish Krueger by taking away his short wave set, but, with the help of staff in the Patient Advocate's office, he prevailed.

"I can still remember listening to Hitler. I couldn't understand what he was saying, but it was frightening. I was four or five years of age. I knew we were at war with people named Germans. I wouldn't have known one if they came up and introduced themselves to me. But I could hear all of these voices on the short wave.

"I've had a short wave radio all of the time that I've been here, except for the time when they wouldn't let me have one because they thought I might use it as a police scanner." he dropped his voice an octave to sound more authoritative, to mimic Oak Ridge's administration— "Only two band radios, AM and FM, and that's it".

At Christmas, 1993, Krueger wanted a pair of headphones for a present. He needed some that had volume controls for each side, so that he could offset his bad ear. I got him a pair and brought them to Oak Ridge. It was the first present he had been given in more than a decade. The headphones were packed in a flower-covered bag because wrapping paper would have been torn apart by Oak Ridge security. Then they were delivered to the ward where Krueger lives. Staff hung onto them until Christmas Day. Never one for delayed gratification, he got a bit testy when I wouldn't tell him what the present was.

"Are they the headphones?" he asked over the phone, shortly after noon on Christmas Eve. "My set broke last night, and unless I have new headphones, the people on the ward are going to have to listen to me playing Radio New Zealand tonight. Last night they had a quite enjoyable selection of Maori Christmas music."

I told him that it was Christmas Eve, that he would have to wait. But he kept at me, and a few minutes later, I relented somewhat.

"The present is supposed to be delivered to your ward today. If you can get it out of them, it's yours."

That made him happy. He thanked me, then tried to pin me down about when I would be visiting over Christmas. I looked out the window of my apartment, and saw the point of land that Krueger lives on being buried by a snow squall. I could think of better things to do at Christmas, but I had to go back.

My own reaction to being locked in Oak Ridge with Krueger varied. Some days, I could walk through Oak Ridge's big wooden doors and the three sets of barred doors at the front gate with no problem. Other times, I broke into a cold sweat, as soon as one of the barred doors slammed shut behind me and I heard the guard turn his big brass key. I carried a couple of tranquillizers in my wallet, and, a couple of times while I talked to Krueger, I succumbed to the urge to go into a washroom and take one.

Krueger understood. He hasn't been given any real treatment in years, but he wishes someone would invent a drug that would make him "normal". LSD was fun, he says, but the drugs that are available today make him feel miserable.

"I've been on most of the phenothiazines. They cause your muscles to stiffen up, your breathing to become laboured, convulsions. You see people on them who walk around all grey, a little bit of drool hanging from their mouths. Those are the people the medication is helping, believe it or not. The problem with most psychotropic medications, up until just recently, is that not only do they inhibit the thought disorders, or whatever the problem is that they're being prescribed to control, but they put you flat on your back. And the way you experience it is like you've got a heavy weight on your chest, time slows down. You might as well be dead, because nothing is really happening. Your appreciation of time is all distorted. Some medications cause hallucinations, rather than clear them up. You give somebody eight milligrams of trilofon and sixty milligrams of millarel, which is a sexual suppressant as well as a major tranquillizer, the two of them in combination with cause hallucinations in most people. You're not supposed to do that. They do it here anyway".

Krueger admits to having given up on medications and drugs years ago, so his pharmaceutical knowledge is a bit rusty. He had a bad time on MOA Inhibitors, a type of anti-anxiety drug that, in their earlier forms, caused violent side effects, especially if patients didn't follow strict dietary restrictions. Most of Krueger's drug treatments were in the 1960s and 1970s, when he was put on them as a member of experimental groups.

"What I would like them to do, of course they won't, not for a while anyway, is give me the medication that I think, I stress, what I think, unlocks the conundrum, the mystery, the riddle, or whatever there is there. When they first came out with the anti-androgen drugs (chemical castration), as far back as the late '60s, I noticed on the bulletin board a notice about chemical castration. That's where they inject something into the ducts of the gonads, the fatty part above the pelvic bone, to block the nerves to the testicles and the penis to prevent erection. Now, of course, everyone thinks that's really primitive, but in the late '60s, it was seen as a breakthrough. It was permanent. Then they started working on something that would do the job, the same kind of drug, but it could be more scientifically controlled, so that people could get married, have children.

"Several types of drugs have been evolved, but none of the have the permanency of this earlier, more permanent thing." He's now looking into the same kind of implant technology that's being used for birth control. He's scared, however, that he might be left androgenous.

"I'm afraid I might have to send away for a size B cup.No thank you. I have enough problems without turning into something in between."

The other option is to make a life inside. That would mean more contact with people from the outside world, meaningful work, and a comfortable place to sleep. Krueger says he would like them to recreate the Oak Ridge farm, but that's unlikely to happen. Nor, probably, are other patients interested in doing jobs around the hospital or organizing some kind of manufacturing business. There are workshops in Oak Ridge, but the brighter inmates need to be managers if they're going to be happy with their work in the long term. Psychopaths are natural managers, and, probably, account for a large percentage of the people in politics. They get frustrated when they're put to work banging pieces of lumber together or refinishing antique furniture for the staff. They quit and watch TV all day, or, worse, make trouble.

Bored patients are often responsible for attacks on guards, who, in earlier years, used towels to protect themselves. Through the 1990s, Oak Ridge was the focus of an Ontario Provincial Police investigation into the "choking out" of patients. Guards would whip a towel around a violent patient's neck, twist it to cut off blood to the brain, and catch the patient when he collapsed. Krueger supported chokeout as reasonable force to keep Oak Ridge secure.

"I have seen patients choked into unconsciousness, and it was usually done after one hell of a donnybrook where the staff were at risk along with everyone else. There could be only one or two patients, and there would be fifteen staff members trying to subdue them. You would have a hall full of people trying to subdue the fighters. They didn't have time for such niceties as using a towel to choke someone. When a guy was approaching the staff with a butcher knife or a shank, the guy would be walking up the corridor with a home-made knife, whistling cheerfully as he headed toward the supervisor because he's going to cut some carotids. And it didn't matter to him if the supervisor bled to death. It might improve the colour scheme of the ward, the red in with all that blue and green.

"The buttons would be pushed. Back in the old days, it was a lot more exciting to watch than it is now. Today, on the P.A., all you hear is, "attention, attention". Ward 01 alert. You would see all of the attendants running toward the ward, all out of breath, out of shape, but they wouldn't do anything. In the old days, I nicknamed them the barn dances, because all the staff would go from the wards, leaving the wards totally deserted, and they would just run like crazy. Instead of just two or three arriving out of breath, out of condition, you now had thirty people in the same passage. The sheer weight of numbers pushed the people who go their first into the fray, and finally the sheer desperation prevailed, and the patient went down.

"They would use their arm around the throat to put the patient out. I never saw the staff injure the patient any more than was absolutely necessary to reduce the threat. If a patient struggled to the point of unconsciousness, the hold would be maintained. If he calmed down, they would let up on the hold, but the patient would still be securely held because some guys, as soon as they felt the pressure relax, they would start up again. I'm not a defender of the staff at the time or an apologist, but I have seen a lot of incidents, and my personal judgement is that I cannot think of one minute when the staff was doing anything more than was desirable to secure the situation. A lot of people would disagree with that.

"I've seen a patient being choked out assuming an expression of total stupidity before he passed out, and then because he had urinated after he passed out, which is a common human reaction, they gave him the boots."

"I have never been beaten. With the staff, it gets to the point where, when you see them shifting their chairs, you disappear. In the meantime, you treat strategic staff with a lot of politeness, a lot of respect, then when a lower staff person is saying 'that no good bastard Krueger...', the boss is saying 'what are you talking about? He always treats me with respect and dignity'."

In the years after the Kerr murder, life at Oak Ridge was usually uneventful. The government slapped a garnishee on Krueger's $113 monthly provincial allowance, chopping it by $6.50 because he had illegally collected it while he was in jail. He had time to think about cannibalism ("I've been wondering what it would be like," he said, one day as a child at another visitor centre table threw a tantrum). He makes up jokes starring "an old serial killer" that usually end with the murderer getting his comeuppance on some mouthy kid, and told them to me.

Usually, he just listened to radio talk shows, agreeing with most of the tirades of their hosts and callers.

In 1977, he was punished for clowning around. Staff were sick of his witticisms, and they ordered him to stop telling jokes.

"One thing that you learn here fast is that you don't joke about your illness in front of a psychiatrist. The wonderful way to get written up is 'no appreciation for the consequence of his crime'."

There were frightening times for Krueger. Off and on, there were rumours that Hamill and his friends were going to get him. In June, 1994, a psychotic patient who had refused to take his medication broke the end off a spoon and stabbed Krueger in the head while the men on the ward were eating breakfast.

Krueger was given first aid and a stitch to close the wound, but nothing else came of the attack. It probably had nothing to do with the Kerr murder, but it shook Krueger for several months.

There are no longer tours of students and reporters through his ward, no more open houses where he could pretend he was a tour guide while people from Penetanguishene wandered the wards, looking for famous faces.

"That's one thing that I agree with. We live here, and how would you feel if somebody, a bunch of nursing students wandered through your home. People are sitting on the toilet, answering the call of nature, which is common, and all of a sudden, there's all these people going gawk, gawk, gawk. I resent not being asked, too. In the old days, when they used to have the open houses back here in the '60s, we used to co-operate with the staff by playing up on the public's anxieties and fears.

"There was a fella by the name of Hunt who had a small piece of bamboo that he would pretend to use as a fishing rod. He would tie a piece of line from it to a goldfish that he put in his toilet and as people would go by and say, 'look at the crazy patient fishing'. Then they'd always inquire 'are you catching anything?' He'd pull the fish out and say 'yes, isn't Penetang tap water wonderful?'"

Of course, there was always enough controversy to keep the pot boiling.

In the spring of 1993, Gord Fleming, a long-time attendant at Oak Ridge, was sitting on a chair on his ward, talking to another staffer, when a patient reached over and grabbed his crotch. Fleming's instant reaction was to push the inmate away and tell him to "fuck off". Management decided the shove and the curse was physical abuse. Fleming, whose wife had recently died, was suspended for three twelve-hour shifts, losing a week's pay. I asked George Kytayko, the mental health centre's administrator, what he would have done, but he dodged the question: "None of us are in that situation. It's hard to say what actually occurred and what should have been done."

Fellow attendants took up a collection to cover Fleming's lost wages. They wore black armbands in protest. Morale, already low, dropped a few more degrees.

In March, 1989, the anger at Oak Ridge erupted in a wildcat strike. Nurses and attendants locked out managers for twenty-four hours after management ordered them to wear rubber gloves while handing out cutlery. Then, seven months later, after Krueger had been transferred to Brockville, a much nastier strike began that lasted three days. Security staff chained the front door shut with handcuffs and leg irons. Patients were locked in their cells. This strike was part of a province-wide disruption by jail guards. Oak Ridge attendants and provincial jail guards belong to the same union.

This time, the managers fought back. After huddling at the nearby regional hospital, they brought in police who used bolt cutters to get the manacles off the main door. It was the first time in a decade that the attendants had lost a takeover action.

After managers retook the hospital, they held a victory party at the most expensive hotel in the area. It was not a stepping stone to better labour relations. Then, a few weeks later, the hospital administration presented the union with a bill for $1,000 for the manacles and leg irons that were ruined when the hospital was re-taken.

Meanwhile, the patients got on the phone to Legal Aid, which pledged the money needed to fight a lawsuit against the union. The patients then hired a blue-chip Toronto law firm to file a claim for more than $3 million.

In November, 1993, the five members of the nursing staff who had been reprimanded by the College of Nurses for leading the illegal strikes were let off the hook by a three-judge Divisional Court panel, who, essentially, said the strike was a union-management dispute and not something that need to be dealt with by the College.

Two years later, however, the guards' own union ended up settling with the eleven patients who filed the lawsuit against the Ontario Public Service Employees Union and its Oak Ridge local executive. The attendants were furious when OPSEU handed over $45,000 to be divided between the inmates. Most got $4,500, but since Krueger was in Brockville during one of the strikes, he only got $2,250.

Garry Lenehan, who led members of the Ontario Public Service Employees Union during the two walk-outs and who was named in the lawsuit, tried to block the payouts. For a while, he considered leading a decertification drive and joining another public sector union. "As a taxpayer, I'm paying their room and board and now I'm supposed to give them spending money. We walked out in 1989 over legitimate security issues. There were fifty-four items that we negotiated with the government. If Queen's Park agreed that we had reasonable grievances, why are we paying money to these guys? The patients are showing more wisdom than the union. I was never consulted, I was never given may day in court. I didn't even hear about it until I read it in the *Toronto Star*," Lenehan told me.

Local merchants were happier. Several stereo dealers in the Penetanguishene area said patients ordered new sound systems. As well, staff at Oak Ridge told me that the number of pizza deliveries at the maximum security institution rose dramatically.

Some of the patients who organized the lawsuit said they deserved the money because security staff violated their rights by locking them in their cells during the four days of work stoppage.

"They treated us with nothing but contempt," said Krueger, who filed the original application for Legal Aid. "They used us as pawns in negotiations, then said that our concerns didn't matter."

These days, though, the cost of defending a lawsuit, especially against people who had the legal aid plan paying for some of the best lawyers in the country, is staggering. OPSEU believed it came out ahead by paying off the Oak Ridge patients. When I talked with a spokesperson for the union, she said OPSEU officials believed it would cost them more to defend themselves in court than it would to give the money to the inmates.

I profited from the lawsuit, although somewhat indirectly. While I was visiting Krueger at Oak Ridge one day in the summer of 1995, he told me to go to a local radio repair shop.

There was something there for me. Ed Webster, a tinkerer who repaired antique radios, had restored a 1940s-vintage console model. It was beautiful. The pine cabinet had been cleaned, the tubes had been replaced, and the sound quality was terrific. The radio had everything that Krueger would want in a hi-fi. It picks up three shortwave bands and AM. The gift was a wedding present. I had been married the summer before, but Krueger had no money for a present. This bothered him. Things have to be done right, just as Mother told him. The short-wave sits in my study. Sometimes, late at night, Krueger calls to tell me that some whacked-out American militia group is broadcasting. It makes for a bizarre evening's recreation, listening to the crazy talk about the Trilateral Commission and the New World Order coming from the short wave, and knowing that Krueger is sitting in his cell, listening, too.

As for the rest of the money, he spent most of it on other people, buying take-out food for patients on his ward, lending them money that he didn't expect to be paid back, buying them presents. Krueger can be a very good friend, unless he decides to hit you over the head with a pipe wrench, rape you and carve you up.

His gift to me came as a flurry of hostile press articles slammed the union for buckling under to inmate pressure. Talk radio hosts went wild with the story. *Readers Digest* picked up on it, running a short item in a monthly section that lists public-sector foulups. Looking back, the union probably did save money, and, if the case had gone to court in a rather embarrassing trial, it would have been stuck with higher legal costs and, possibly, a bigger judgement against it. OPSEU was hamstrung by the fact that Oak Ridge is a hospital, and you can't go around locking up sick people in their rooms for days on end. The fact that most of the patients are killers can't, legally, get the union off the hook.

After a few months, anger over the payouts died down. Then, in the summer of 1996, an Ontario government employee gave me a list of the more notorious killers in Oak Ridge and the amount of money they receive from the Canada Pension Plan disability program. Because they are incarcerated at an

Ontario psychiatric hospital, they can bank the money, since psychiatric institutions do not charge user fees. Jail inmates don't qualify for the disability money and can't get old age pensions or Canada Pension when they turn sixty-five.

On Ward 04 alone, Canada Pension benefits to the twenty patients total more than $10,000 a month. This is a fairly conservative estimate, and the amount may be twice as much. About 75 per cent of the twenty inmates on Oak Ridge's Ward 01 collect monthly Canada Pension Plan disability payments ranging from about $200 to $800 a month. The program started paying long-term psychiatric patients in 1982. Federal officials say there's nothing they can do to prevent Oak Ridge inmates from collecting Canada Pension Plan benefits. Because most of the institution's patients were found not guilty by reason of insanity, they're not covered by rules that prevent prison inmates from receiving pensions.

"If they qualify for CPP disability, we're obliged to pay them," Cathy Trim, senior communications officer, income security program, at Human Resources Canada, told me. "They get it, just as any other Canadian who qualifies gets it. We have to go by the letter of the law," she said.

Another bonanza seemed to arrive in the spring of 1996, when OPSEU went on a province-wide strike. Rather than risk another employee takeover at Oak Ridge, managers and medical staff stayed inside the building for the duration of the strike, sleeping on cots. Their financial windfall came immediately; one doctor collected more than $50,000 in overtime during the month-long strike, and managers made nearly as much. The work wasn't too onerous. Psychologists used some of the time to cross country ski on the grounds of the institutions.

The patients called reporters to complain, and began planning another lawsuit. There were inconveniences: the canteen that normally supplies inmates with cigarettes was closed during the strike. Meals, made at other hospitals and shipped through the picket lines, came in late and were sometimes cold. Recreation programs at the institution's pool and gymnasium were cancelled, and inmates got laid off from their jobs at Oak Ridge's workshops.

Krueger spent most of the strike sedated. He would be so stoned when he called that I could hardly understand what he was saying. The changes in Oak Ridge obviously troubled him. He phoned me a lot. My monthly bill, already staggering, rose by about $100.

"We're stuck on our wards all day long," Krueger told me. "We don't even get out of here to eat. The tension here is rising every day. There could easily be a riot."

That summer, word got out that the Ontario health ministry paid the wages of six security staff so that two inmates of the Oak Ridge could go on a day trip to pick strawberries. Garry Lenehan, back as president of the Ontario Public Service Employees Union local that represents security staff at Oak Ridge, told me the cost of the excursion was more than $1,000, although managers later said the cost was less than half that. Word came back from Queen's Park to cancel the annual Oak Ridge boat tour, some fishing trips that were planned for inmates, and a sort of sidewalk sale that was planned for late summer inside the institution. Managers scrambled to dampen down the public outrage.

Through all those little crises, my phone kept ringing, with that cheery voice telling me the latest gossip. Over the years, the extra cost of the phone bill became part of my regular household expenses. We talk for hours every month about the events in the news, my life working on Parliament Hill, the latest atrocities committed by the Oak Ridge kitchen. We used to talk about the Romanovs, about the finding of their bodies and the funeral that was planned for the former Russian royal family. It was an obsession that I never understood. Then, one day, I got it. Five young children, once beautiful, rich and full of potential, screaming and dying in a basement in Ekaterinburg. One more mask had fallen away, one more vile fantasy revealed.

In the end, nothing's Krueger's fault.

Not the killings of the kids. Wayne Mallette, Gary Morris and Carole Voyce died in a series of accidents. And accidents can happen to anyone. Dennis Kerr was killed at the Brockville Psychiatric Hospital in 1992 in an act of mercy, not an act of rage and lust. And, after all of those killings, the courts had said Peter Woodcock, or David Michael Krueger, was not guilty by reason of insanity. Not guilty. Didn't do it. Accident. Incident. Tragedy. Never a crime committed by this strange little man.

And with Bruce Hamill, it's the same. Poor Mrs. Wentzlaff was stabbed to death on her front lawn in Ottawa because Hamill had an organic brain disease, not because Hamill was a miserable young man with a taste for heavy drugs. When he helped Mike Krueger kill Dennis Kerr, it was that brain disease at work again. Not guilty by reason of insanity. Not culpable. Fished in.

That's the way Krueger tells it. And, as I leave the Oak Ridge visitors' centre, Krueger looks at a Childfind poster of missing kids. He smiles, points, and says, "that one, that one, and that one."

Sources

Barker, E.T., The Penetanguishene Program: A Personal Review (MS 1978).

Barker, E.T, and M.F. Buck, LSD in a coercive milieu therapy program. *Canadian Psychiatric Association Journal*, 14: 355-359 (1969).

Barker, E. T., and M. H. Mason, The Hundred Day Hate-In: A stubborn attempt at staffless milieu therapy. Presented to the Fall Meeting of the Ontario Psychiatric Association, Oct. 5, 1968.

Barker, E.T., and M.H. Mason, The Insane Criminal as Therapist. *Canadian Journal of Corrections* Vol. 10, 553-561.

Barker, E.T., and M.H. Mason, Buber Behind Bars. *Canadian Psychiatric Association Journal*, 13:1 (1968).

Barker, E.T., M.H. Mason, and J. Wilson, Defence-Disrupting Therapy. *Canadian Psychiatric Association Journal*, 14:4 (1969).

Barker, E.T., Protective pairings in Treatment Milieux: Handcuffs for Mental Patients (undated Ms).

Bickley, Claire, Penetang: A warehouse of human souls. (*Toronto Sun*, Oct. 18, 1986)

Bourrie, Mark: Oak Ridge centre now hiring women (*Globe and Mail*, Nov. 21, 1983); Oak Ridge wedding is "waste of public money": union says (*Midland Times*, May 10, 1989); Scrap hospital, ex-psychiatric patients demand (*Toronto Star*, Jan. 8, 1990); Prison-or-hospital debate stirs passion at Oak Ridge (*Toronto Star*, Feb. 20, 1990, Insight); Why psychopathic murderers are allowed back on the streets (*Toronto Star*, June 6, 1990); Psychiatric nurse suspended for warding off inmate's attack (*Toronto Star*, May 5, 1993); Oak Ridge suspension of nurse protested (*Toronto Star*, May 14, 1993).

Boyd, Barry, with Dan Parle, Dr. Boyd remembers his early years at MHCP. *Entre Nous*, March, 1990.

Canadian Press, Psychiatric hospital gets tough talking new chief. July 25, 1994.

Crawford, Trish, Why are we putting mentally ill behind bars? (*Toronto Star*, Sept. 18, 1988).

Cunningham, Alison, Brockville hospital patient found slain (*Ottawa Citizen*, July 14, 1991).

Flavelle, Dana, Poor mental patients ruled entitled to $149 monthly (*Toronto Star*, Sept. 1, 1988)

Hardy, Eldon, *Noble Sheet*, Oak Ridge Patients' Infosheet, July, 1989.

Hardy, Eldon, et al., *Amended Statement of Claim, Hardy et al. vs. James Clancy, Ontario Public Service Emplyee's Union, et al.* Ontario Court of Justice, Court File No. 48355/90. April 20, 1990.

Harris, Grant T., and Marnie E. Rice, Reducing Violence in Institutions: Maintaining Behaviour Change. In R. DeV. Peters, R.J. McMahon, and V.L. Quinsey (Eds.) *Aggression and Violence Through the Lifespan.* New York: Sage, 1992.

Harris, G.T, M.E. Rice and C.A. Cormier, *Violent recidivism among psychopaths and non-psychopaths treated in a therapeutic environment.* Penetanguishene Mental Health Centre Research Reports 6:1 (1989).

Henton, Darcy: 'It is one frustrating ordeal': Criminally insane facing long wait for review hearings (*Toronto Star*, July 19, 1990); The danger of opening the doors (*Toronto Star*, June 24, 1993); City angered by patients' release. MDs fail in asessing insane offenders, probe told (*Toronto Star*, Oct. 23, 1993); Mental hospital under fire after Brockville slaying (*Toronto Star*, Dec. 30, 1993)

Hollobon, Joan, My therapist, the Psychopath. *Globe and Mail Magazine*, March 18, 1967.

Kershaw, Anne, Psychopathy begins at home: prison expert (*Kingston Whig-Standard*, Aug. 30, 1983)

Lynch, D.O., Some Observations on the Criminally Insane With Special Reference to Those Charged With Murder. *Ontario Journal of Neuropsychiatry*, 1937, 12:39-52.

MacCallum, G.A., History of the Hospital for the Insane (Formerly the Military and Naval Depot), Penetanguishene. *Ontario Historical Society Journal*, 1912.

MacLeod, Ian, Predator: the horror that was Joseph Fredericks (*Ottawa Citizen*, Feb. 14, 1993)

Meunck, Morton, The genesis of Oak Ridge: a look at the early history of forensic services in Ontario. *Entre Nous*, Dec., 1990.

Matas, Robert, Outrage prompts castration proposal for sex offenders (*Globe and Mail*, Jan. 15, 1990)

Ottawa Citizen (no byline), Pair ruled insane in brutal murder of patient (Dec. 15, 1992)

Psychiatric Patient Advocate Office, *A Guide to Psychiatric Patients' Rights.* Toronto: Queen's Printer, 1992.

Platiel, Rudy, Criminally insane lack care, official says (Globe and Mail, Oct. 10, 1987)

Quinsey, V.L., The long term management of the mentally disordered offender. In S.J. Hucker, C.D. Webster and M. Ben-Aro, (Eds.), *Mental Disorder and Criminal Responsibility* (pp 137-155). Toronto: Butterworths, 1981.

Quinsey, Vernon L., The Ontario Reformatory at Penetanguishene, 1882. *Canada's Mental Health*, Dec., 1992.

Rice, Marney E., and Grant T. Harris, Ontario's Maximum Security Hospital at Penetanguishene: Past, Present and Future. (undated Ms)

Rice, Marney E., Grant T. Harris and Catherine Cormer, An Evaluation of a Maximum Security Therapeutic Community for Psychopaths and Other Mentally Disordered Offenders. *Law and Human Behavior*, 16:4, Nov. 4, 1992.

Rice, Marney, Grant T. Harris and Vernon L. Quinsey, A Follow-Up of Rapists Assessed in a Maximum Security Psychiatric Institution. *Journal of Interpersonal Violence*, 5:4, Dec. 1990, 425-448.

Rice, Marney E., Grant T. Harris, Donna Sutherland, James Levesque, Principles regarding treatment of patients in psychiatric institutions. *Canada's Mental Health*, Dec. 1990.

Rice, Marney E., Grant T. Harris, Donna Sutherland, James Levesque, A Guide to the Legal Rights and Responsibilities of Patients in Psychiatric Institutions. MHCP publication, undated manuscript.

Rice, Marnie E., Vernon Quinsey, and Grant T. Harris, Sexual Recidivism Among Child Molesters Released From a Maximum Security Institution. *Journal of Consulting and Clinical Psychology*, 59:3.

Ward, Bruce, Killer lives in an alien world. (*Ottawa Citizen*, Dec. 11, 1992); Killer incurably insane, court told. (*Ottawa Citizen*, Dec. 12, 1992); Accused saw role in murder as career move, psychiatrist says. (*Ottawa Citizen*, Dec. 15, 1992); A chilling tale of murder; Killer's twisted mind set schedule for sacrificial death. (*Ottawa Citizen*, Dec. 16, 1992)

Wallace, Norman, The Criminally Insane at Guelph. *Ontario Journal of Neuropsychiatry*, December, 1925, 72-77.

Williams, Norman F., and Joan M. MacDonald, Irked by Lenehan's remarks (*Midland Free Press*, May 24, 1984)

Withrow, W.H. (Ed.), The Prison System of Ontario. *Methodist Magazine*, January-June, 1994, p. 99.

Valpy, Michael, Naked in the Box. *Globe and Mail Magazine*, December, 1968.

CPSIA information can be obtained at www.ICGtesting.com
Printed in the USA
LVOW01s0754160314

377490LV00005B/26/P